The Thirteenth Overdose

Parenting my son through FASD and addiction

Ruth Spencer

The Thirteenth Overdose:
Parenting my son through FASD and Addiction

Author: Ruth Spencer
Published by: A.F.S.Books

Copyright © 2021 A.F.S.Books

All rights reserved. No portion of this book, except for brief review, may be reproduced, stored in a retrieval system, or transmitted in any form or by any means without written permission of the author.

Cover Design: Tim Spencer
Book Design: Jim Bisakowski bookdesign.ca
Editors: Jo Ann Lorimer and Rachel J. Peterson

ISBN: 978-0-9948892-3-2—Book
ISBN: 978-0-9948892-4-9—e-Book

1. Fetal Alcohol Spectrum Disorder
2. Disability > special needs
3. Addiction > rehabilitation
4. Family & Relationships > adoption
5. Justice > Legal System and Corrections

Author contact
P.O. Box 21088, Duncan, B. C., V9L 1P8

4ruth.spencer@gmail.com

This book is a memoir. It presents the author's present recollections of past experiences. Some names have been changed and some dialogue has been modified.

Margaret Mary McAully 1940 – 2020

*For my unforgettable friend,
affectionately known to all as Sunni
because of her sunny disposition and constant smile.*

Also by Ruth Spencer

The Burning: Parenting my son through adoption, FASD, and suicide

Contents

A Preface 6

Introductions .8

2014 – 2015 10

2016. 48

2017. 106

2018. 166

2019 – Emails 229

Appendix I
    Celebrating St. Nicholaas 234

Appendix II
    Disabilities of Fetal Alcohol Spectrum
    Disorder 239

Appendix III
    Glossary of Acronyms 241

Appendix IV
    Recipes from My Dutch Sister-in-law . 242

Appendix IV
    Life in the Trenches 244

A Preface

for the parents of those adult children who are struggling with Fetal Alcohol Spectrum Disorder and addiction.

There are no easy formulas that will lead to success. As a parent of three with FASD, I can only share with you what has worked for me.

You will find yourself associated with numerous government ministries and agencies, and their constant changes of junior staff. Try not to deal with subordinates; when you can, go directly to the top.

Make every effort to get your adult child onto Disability Assistance and fight for irreversible Rent Direct.* Then you can relax on wet, cold nights, knowing he has a roof.

Become involved with the local food bank or soup kitchen. If possible, get your adult child connected there as well. It really helps to know she is eating more or less regularly. And even if your child refuses to accept this support, if *you* are there, you can hear how she is doing through her friends. You won't have to ask—the street people will tell you soon enough!

If your child is involved with the legal system and Corrections, is penniless, and is willing to accept help, check out the Legal Aid lawyers and get the best available. Always be present in the courtroom; mothers and fathers are very rare and very welcome. And remember, the Crown is *not* the enemy. Medical reports, records, and other important information will stay in the legal system unless someone, probably you, sees that it moves across the great divide into Corrections.

Have no expectations.
No matter what happens, offer love and acceptance.

*Rent Direct: a pre-authorized direct debit rent payment plan available through the B.C. Government

Introductions

First, the book.

It's really a journal.

During my son's last few years of addiction, when he was either living on the streets, using and overdosing, or living in prison, detoxing and recovering, the writing of our shared experiences was my pathway to survival.

Second, the family.

Let's start with the author—I'm old and worn out. My husband, Peter, died ten years ago.

Our children are all in their forties now, except for the eldest, our only daughter Kathleen, who has just celebrated her fiftieth birthday. I can't believe my very first baby is already fifty.

The boys are James, our firstborn, married to Elaine; Zan, three years younger, married to Bedelia; Tim, third son, who keeps my life interesting, and Alex, our youngest, who died in 2002 when he was twenty-five. Peter and I adopted Alex, Tim, and Kathleen without knowing that all three had been born with Fetal Alcohol Spectrum Disorder.

Third, the next generation.

I am Oma to eight precious grandchildren, one of whom is genetically linked.

Alex and his girlfriend, Cricket, produced my first granddaughter, Kaitlyn, now in her early twenties. Cricket has since married; she and Clay have two more children. Zan and Bedelia have three: one birthed, one adopted, one fostered. Tim has twin boys, now in elementary school.

Fourth, our support people:

Mary Grace, originally my counselor, now my best friend and very popular with my children and grandchildren.

My brother Bruce and his wife, Alana.

Volunteer supervisor Anne.

Uri at The Doggy Bath.

Sister Marianna, who was Tim's first social worker.

Cousins Norma, Elizabeth and Van.

Basil, the best of several probation officers.

Jill at the food bank.

Lawyers Stefano and Skye.

Tim's Team, a group of adult FASD associates who have known us for years.

Tim's favourite nurse, Helen, who works with the homeless population.

Sterling, Mike, and Rashelle, Tim's friends.

Tim's other street friends. Nice kids, and don't even try to remember all their names. I can't.

2014 – 2015

Sunday, November 2, 2014

Tim just phoned me; he and his girlfriend have been fighting again.

This is nothing new. My son and his girlfriend are constantly quarreling. And it's not always discreet verbal disagreement, either—I've heard them in action, and they can get downright nasty. They swear at each other with unkind remarks and name-calling. Sometimes, although not in front of me, there is physical violence on both sides. It wouldn't be so bad if they fought in private but they do battle in front of their children.

The twins never fight. When Mommy and Daddy start arguing they plead, "Don't fight. Please don't fight."

When their parents reach the stage of yelling at each other, the two little ones hold hands and hide.

Whenever their fighting gets truly out of hand, as it apparently did tonight, this couple separates. The tall, blond girlfriend insists my son has to leave. It's *her* house; he has his own place, a seldom used apartment.

But now there seems to be a major change. Tim is choosing to leave and he doesn't want to return. He says it's bad for the kids to see their parents attacking each other. He plans to phone his youngsters every evening and visit them twice a week at my place.

Monday, November 10, 2014

The girlfriend has decided her sons can't be anywhere near Daddy unless another adult is there to supervise. I get to be the supervisor.

This should be a workable solution for all of us. Tim and I function well together. The little boys have had lots of babysitting time with me, both at their own home and at my place. And, in spite of the ups and downs in this couple's relationship, the girlfriend and I are friends.

Monday, December 1, 2014

For me, this was a perfect day. The twins were here for several hours. The weather was gorgeous; we could go out for a walk. And both Tim and his girlfriend were in good moods, arriving and leaving at the times previously promised.

The little boys have their mother's blond curls and their father's creamy brown skin. I think they are absolutely beautiful!

When they are playing on the floor, digging through the old toy box, my little grandsons remind me of Zan, Tim, and Alex who played with the same toys thirty-five years ago. My three youngest had birthdays only ten months apart; it was almost like having triplets. And now we have real twins!

Wednesday, January 7, 2015

The girlfriend is still angry because Tim left without her consent. She has dealt with her problem by serving him through the courts.

Over a shared cup of coffee in my kitchen she told me she would be demanding full custody of the little boys and legalized supervision of their time with their father.

But yesterday when they went to court, the judge said, "Sorry, it doesn't work this way. Mediation, rather than applying for custody, is the first step."

They both agreed to see a mediator, and they both signed.

I'm doubtful about mediation for these guys. It's supposed to be used to resolve disputes; to do that, the mediator helps you work out what your basic disagreements really are. And it's supposed to be focused on the true needs of the two people involved. But these two operate on such different levels I suspect they will never finish off the first bit: naming their problems. At the end of the day they are supposed to design a settlement. Can't see that happening, either.

Thursday, January 8, 2015

First thing this morning Tim went, as instructed, to the court-appointed mediator. He was told his girlfriend had been there two months ago. In spite of her signature at court she had already refused mediation services. She said she was not willing to compromise.

Tim had to go back to the courthouse and do the paperwork to serve her. He agreed the children should live with their mother and he was demanding mediation, shared custody, and visiting rights written in stone.

He was helped by a first class duty counsel. I'm hoping to get her lined up for the next court date when Tim and his girlfriend end up as participants in the legal system. That's what is supposed to happen, even if mediation works out. They're setting a date for a custody hearing at the end of January but the way the courts are backed up, the hearing—if it happens—could be a year from now.

The girlfriend has already been served. This evening she brought the papers to show me, burst into tears, and said, "I don't want this."

But mediation will be going ahead unless the girlfriend can prove Tim is a deadbeat dad beforehand. She is hopeful.

I'm feeling seriously caught in the middle.

Friday, January 9, 2015

The court-appointed mediator is enormously busy, with a long waiting list, but obtaining an outside mediator is complicated and usually expensive. You have to make your own arrangements.

I suggested seeking out an aboriginal mediator since Tim has

First Nations status and for him it would be a free service, but he said, "No!"

He had talked to them once before and they were eager to help him until they heard his girlfriend was white. Then it was raised eyebrows and negative comments. Tim says he doesn't want to expose his girlfriend to racism—it wouldn't be fair.

I said, "But you need help to get this matter organized, and Tribes has got some outstanding mediators."

He won't use them. I raised a gentleman.

And the girlfriend won't do anything about mediation until it is forced upon her because at the moment she has everything her own way. She has decided Tim won't be allowed to see his sons without outside supervision. No more playing with Daddy at Oma's place.

This isn't about me, but it still feels as if a friend has suddenly turned against me.

Monday, January 12, 2015

Tim just sent me an email, and I'm going to save it. Not sure why. Tim and his girlfriend have had years of battles and separations. Nothing is different but I have a nasty feeling this time.

> Morning Mom
>
> Just talked to my girlfriend. She has to work tomorrow, and she asked Tabby from Daycare to watch the boys since I'm not allowed to be with them according to her. Cost is $70 for the day. I said I could help with $35. I was hoping the last of my Christmas money from you could cover. I think there is $45 left??? If that sounds OK, one of us can pick up a check from you later today.
>
> Not impressed by her. So basically no more visits till mediation is figured out. Really sucks. Glad I am working today—that helps.

Wednesday, January 14, 2015

The girlfriend appeared yesterday morning with her hand out and not a word to me apart from, "Hello."

The little boys have been asking to visit Tabby for ages. She was their day care person when they were tiny; they haven't seen her since they started preschool. They wanted to show Tabby their Christmas presents but their mother was busy and considered a visit to the old daycare unimportant.

Last night when Tim thanked me for the money, he said, "A whole day with Tabby was the nicest possible late Christmas present for the twins."

Wednesday, January 28, 2015

Court this morning to line up duty counsel and set a date for the custody hearing. The cumbersome wheels of the legal system went slowly grinding along. Nothing else happened.

There is no organization in our courthouse. Never a suggestion of stand in line or take a number. Tim and I were among the cluster of clients waiting outside a door for the duty counsel when an elite lawyer came barging through, with, "I need an office, please!" The fellow being duty counsel had to shift to a different room.

And didn't the girlfriend, who had been chatting with her sister in the corridor, scuttle along behind him and get in before us. Thwarted! We couldn't go to the same duty counsel; it would have been considered a conflict of interest. We would have to wait for the other duty who was due to start work later in the day. The judge wouldn't see Tim, not even to set a date for a future hearing, unless he had legal representation.

As it turned out, we didn't have to hang around for long. The girlfriend's official lawyer is away enjoying a holiday. Her duty counsel only had to ask the judge for a two week extension. Tim signed the request—afterwards he was sorry he had given in so quickly—and we left.

I thought the girlfriend's parents had paid for a lawyer for her but apparently she is using free Legal Aid. For family matters, Legal Aid is available under two conditions: you have to be poor and your children have to be at risk. Poor as he is, my son refuses to lie. Therefore he can't get Legal Aid; he's stuck with whoever is the assigned duty counsel.

Saturday, January 31, 2015

It's cold and dark and horribly early but the coffee is brewing. A nasty dream woke me up—something about being in court with a gorilla for a judge.

I can't believe we are back in the legal system. Although Tim hasn't been involved in any crimes since he moved in with this girlfriend, he was either in trouble with the law, in jail, or on probation from age seventeen to age thirty-seven. Until recently this girlfriend has been a good influence.

My coffee is ready.

Thursday, February 12, 2015

Tim and I went to the courthouse to sign up for Legal Aid.

At last!!!

I've been trying to persuade him to go but he refused because you have to say your children are in jeopardy. He wouldn't say it, not only to protect his girlfriend but also to keep his sons out of foster care.

But when we were last at court, the duty counsel, who could see the girlfriend was getting everything entirely her own way, said: "You need to apply for Legal Aid."

Even Tim noticed he wasn't being treated fairly but he wouldn't start his application without my help.

I phoned the lawyer who had already guided Tim through the serving of his girlfriend last month after she had refused to go to mediation. The lawyer said she remembered him. She would take him as a client if he was approved for Legal Aid.

She added, "In the absence of Legal Aid, any lawyer's fees would be $250 per hour, with a $5000 retainer fee."

At the Legal Aid office we got an exceptionally helpful First Nations secretary, who did the forms with Tim. When she asked the bad question: "Are the kids in danger?"

Tim said, "Sure."

"And what is that danger?"

Tim muttered, "In danger of not seeing their father."

I said, "They aren't in any physical danger so this is complicated. His girlfriend sometimes says half of the truth, and it twists things around."

I had examples. Tim used to phone the little boys every night but their mother doesn't want any more contact.

She tells them, "Daddy won't be phoning," instead of saying, "I don't want Daddy to talk to you." Being told the truth would make this easier for the children.

I said, "Tim doesn't want his youngsters to feel in any way responsible for this separation."

I didn't want to say, in front of him, "She is letting the kids believe Daddy left because they were bad," but the secretary got it instantly.

Another example from my daughter, Kathleen: whenever she met Tim and the little ones downtown they greeted her with, "Hi, Aunty Kathleen!" and hugs all round.

But now, when she meets them with their mother, the kids duck quickly out of sight behind Mommy.

Tim said, "Oh that's just her. They pick up attitude from her." Exactly! He doesn't see this as twisting the little ones' thinking but I do.

The secretary at Legal Aid said Tim would hear in five business days whether or not he was accepted. He called me a few moments ago. The same lady had just phoned him (at night!) to say he's been approved for Legal Aid, his lawyer already knows, and he should connect with the lawyer tomorrow and make an appointment.

Wednesday, March 18, 2015

We are going to have a late celebration of my birthday. Elaine, our family event coordinator, set the location, did the planning, sent the invitations, and immediately ran into complications with Tim's girlfriend. All three were coming; then it was just the two children. She promised to drive her little boys up island and drop them off at my cousin's home; then she said she wouldn't. They could travel with Mary Grace; then they could travel with Mary Grace only if their mother came too.

And the conditions! The future trial was not to be mentioned. The family must agree to keep the peace. No photographs of her twins were allowed.

I checked with Tim. He desperately wanted to see his kids and felt he could cope with his girlfriend's conditions.

He said, "But why does she want to come? I predict she'll try to get us back into a relationship!"

Monday, March 23, 2015

My birthday party was harmonious. The children thoroughly enjoyed the occasion. The adults cooperated with Tim's girlfriend and made her feel as welcome as we could under the circumstances. She had a good time. She laughed a lot, cracked jokes, and appeared to be on friendly terms with everybody.

No one brought out a camera.

The aunts and uncles and adult cousins made a huge fuss of the twins, whom they hadn't seen or spoken to for three months. Christmas was the last occasion the whole family had been together.

No one mentioned the upcoming trial.

When Mary Grace arrived at the party with the twins and their mother, she gave me a quiet warning: The girlfriend had said she would have to constantly monitor Tim. She did. She stayed with him, unobtrusively, for the whole event.

Tim's siblings, being nervous about the girlfriend's motives and also her button pushing tendencies, decided among themselves to protect him. They continually popped in and out of whichever room he and the five youngsters were using. They were diligent about keeping the peace.

There were a couple of small episodes I found difficult.

Twin Two, unlucky little boy, pooped his pants. He's the one who soaked Tim's lap last Christmas. Both parents, having themselves been bed-wetters into puberty, used to cope with Twin Two lightly. But now his mother is obviously irritated and convinced this whole problem is his father's fault.

I was alone in the living room, snatching a few moments of rest and appreciating a break from the noise when Twin One came upstairs carrying a stuffed cow. He stopped in front of me.

I said, "How are you doing?"

"Fine."

I asked, "Are you getting tired? We'll be going home, soon."

Twin One said, "I don't want to go home. I want to stay here, with Daddy."

After the party, the girlfriend asked Tim, "Why aren't you phoning the boys the way you used to? The no contact order has been lifted."

And, as Tim had expected, she suggested they renew their relationship. He said to me, "I told you!" and asked what I thought.

I said, "I think it would be best for your children if you two put togetherness on hold until your mediation is worked out."

Tim has lost about forty-five pounds since he hasn't been allowed to see his kids. His girlfriend asked if he had lost the weight on purpose. He told her he couldn't eat because he was stressed out.

She said, "So am I."

Tuesday, March 24, 2015

Just contemplating last Sunday's party, and I'm wondering if the girlfriend's emotional quotient could be a bit low. She doesn't seem able to respond to the inner needs of others. If the little boys come in with skinned knees or cut fingers she makes a big fuss over the wound rather than offering comfort to the wounded.

Somehow she has no comprehension of the pain and stress she is now inflicting on her sons. She thinks the boys are better off without their father, apparently not realizing Tim has always been the parent who provides for their emotional needs.

My grandchildren are hurting. They need to see Daddy frequently, without being subjected to dramatic changes of mind or the imposing of difficult conditions.

It's hard for me, too. The girlfriend appears to have lost track of the way she and I used to be friends. She is considerably smarter than me (she has a university degree) but we both used to take pleasure in good coffee and congenial conversations. At least that's what I thought.

Tuesday, April 21, 2015

We've had a slow but significant change. Over the last month, Tim and his girlfriend have been less and less confrontational, and now there is actually some harmony happening. The children are much happier, and their father is seeing them often enough to make him careless about the smooth deceptions of his girlfriend.

Last Friday, he came to my house for supper and to watch the hockey game. At about 6 p.m. he received a text and began to rush around collecting his belongings.

I said, "What's up?"

Tim said, "I have to go." He laughed and added, "That was my girlfriend but she said not to tell you. She asked if I wanted to go to the park with the boys. I can't believe I'm giving up my hockey game!"

"Do you want me to drive you anyplace?"

Tim said, "No. I'm not supposed to tell you this, either, but she and the kids are parked around the corner at the gas station."

The next day he told me the little ones hadn't been there—he was enormously disappointed.

On Sunday I had company at my house for lunch; Kathleen without her dog and Tim with his family. The lunch was Tim's idea. He told his girlfriend, "Oma and Aunty Kathleen are missing the boys." We had a fun, sociable visit, with most of the conversation geared to the youngsters.

I do have concerns about Twin Two. He ignored me while we were eating but later he came into the living room and sat on the sofa close beside me. I put my arm around him. Looking straight ahead, and without a word, he slowly picked up my hand and put it on his stomach and held it there.

My other problem: I'm finding myself having to be careful about what I say when I'm with Tim's girlfriend. We used to be relaxed and comfortable together. Now she seems to be always on the verge of either losing her temper or bursting into tears.

Thursday, April 30, 2015

Anne, a longtime friend of each of the twins' four grandparents, has been approved, by the girlfriend, as a supervisor of Tim and the little boys. Anne and Tim have both been informed but there hasn't been a supervised playdate yet.

I can't understand this whole "supervisor" innovation. Last summer the girlfriend spent hours picking and selling fresh fruit. Tim cared for the children, often at his own apartment, while she was gone. And last year when Mommy was working, it was Tim and me who drove the kids to their swimming and karate lessons. He has photos and selfies, taken at his apartment, of his sons dressed in their cute little karate uniforms waiting for me to come by and pick them up.

What has changed?

The lawyer told me, "The bad part is, while the girlfriend is doing the supervising herself, she is very much in control," and, "She is stopping any independent witnesses from seeing how suitably Tim can parent. In court it could come down to balancing her word against his."

The lawyer and I are both worried about another unpredictable confrontation between these two. According to Tim, who is far from blameless, his girlfriend always starts the battles and uses them to sabotage him later. He has taken Anger Management, and he understands it's best to keep his distance if she tries to annoy him but the problem is she follows him, nagging and haranguing. Apparently she can't stop herself.

Tim's girlfriend would have an entirely different story! But she knew about Tim's FASD, and his addictions, and his various problems with the law, long before she got pregnant and moved in with him. And he knew her. They had travelled in the same crowd for years before they cohabited and, as Tim told me early in the new relationship, "We used to dislike each other. She was always such a goody-goody."

Saturday, May 2, 2015

The manager at Kathleen's building, an elderly man with severe alcohol dependency, is letting the place fall into ruin. He doesn't have regular maintenance done on the roof, or the heat, or the electrical system, or the elevators, or the plumbing, or the communal laundry. Kathleen says all requests for repairs and all complaints by tenants are ignored.

Tim is blessed with unusually sharp hearing. Last week, when he was borrowing Kathleen's vacuum cleaner, he heard her building manager talking to his wife. He caught the name of the building owner.

I went to the office of our MLA, armed with nothing more than one name. With help from the secretary there, an address and a phone number were found. The secretary made an official connection with the building owner. Then we put together a letter and checked it for legalities. I completed the writing, made seventy-five copies and mailed one anonymously to every tenant.

To All Tenants:

The Owner of our building wants anyone who has a complaint to go through the correct process with the Manager, and give him the issues in writing. Be sure to keep a dated copy of your complaint.

If your problem is not resolved appropriately, within a few days, then you should email or write to the Owner of this building, explaining your difficulty. Be polite!

When you contact the Owner, please send a copy of your letter or e-mail to our MLA's office. They are looking into this on our behalf.

This is a message from the Owner: "No one has to feel anxious about getting into trouble for having pointed out problems that don't seem to be taken care of."

I thought for sure Kathleen would phone and tell me about her letter, but not a peep. Then her toilet quit working properly. She *didn't* phone me, full of worries and sure that there was no point complaining because nothing would be done. Instead, she gave the building manager a note about it and he had a satisfactory repairman up there within the week. This was a double miracle! In the past if any repairs were done the manager did the work himself and he did it badly.

I sent an appreciative note off to the MLA's secretary.

He wrote back, "Yes, there has been a definite change in the attitude of the building manager. I had a long talk with him and I have had excellent reports of work getting done."

Tuesday, May 19, 2015

Tim and his girlfriend began "dating" last April, soon after my birthday party. With the arrival of spring, Tim started working regularly and he offered child support. Money made all the difference. She has invited him back into her house and he is delighted to oblige; his little boys are there.

We had a family function in Victoria, last weekend. The occasion was a party celebrating the birth of Zan and Bedelia's oldest. The girlfriend said she would come with Tim and their children. We were all pleased.

But Tim's whole paycheque had gone to groceries for his family. He asked me, "Do you have anything here we could take along as a gift? And could we borrow ten dollars for gas?"

I said, "Sure, I can find something that will make a good present. But this gas money is for your girlfriend, not for you. I think it should be returned."

Tim said, "*She* said it's for me. If I want the boys to go, I have to borrow the money."

Oh well. For years, I've been 'lending' money to these two.

Saturday, May 23, 2015

Tim and his little boys were officially observed/supervised by Anne, at my house. Why did the girlfriend set it up now when the whole family is living together? It was supposed to be 9 a.m. till noon, but Tim called to say they were behind schedule. The kids needed baths and breakfasts before they could leave home.

He usually does the baths and the breakfasts.

Years ago when both parents were working and I had a day with the babies it was always easy to tell which parent had done the morning chores. If Tim was in charge, they were bathed, dressed and fed. If the girlfriend was in charge, they were hungry, wet, rumpled, and still wearing their pyjamas.

Today they were twenty minutes late. I wouldn't have noticed but

Anne thought the visit should now extend to 12:20 p.m. The girlfriend seemed comfortable with this ruling. She brought a notebook and presented it to Anne with a request to "write everything that happens." She came back early but stayed for lunch, allowing the children to have their full three hours with Daddy.

The girlfriend, when asked, told Anne she and Tim were not living together. Tim, when asked, told Anne they were living together on and off, but mostly on. Anne also asked them about their drug and alcohol use. The girlfriend lied: Tim told the truth. Nobody but Anne would ask those kinds of questions!

The girlfriend told Tim she has seen her lawyer and, "We will be working out our problems." But she is telling others, including Anne, she is going to court for full custody.

Sunday, May 31, 2015

A while ago, Tim let an evicted couple, Henry and Isobel, live with him at his apartment. He didn't charge them any rent for the eight to ten weeks they stayed—typical.

When he started living with his girlfriend, he told me there would be a domestic dispute as soon as Henry and Isobel were alone together. Sure enough. They escalated into violence, a neighbour phoned 911, and the apartment was raided by the police. The building manager, in the way of most building managers, sent the couple on their way.

But according to one of the neighbours, the raid happened because Isobel and Henry were dealing crystal meth. Many of the renters who live in Tim's building are not okay, and they build up details until they believe their own stories.

I hope the girlfriend doesn't hear either version. She would believe whichever she thought was the worst and use it against him.

The power in Tim's apartment was turned off because he had lost track of his hydro bill. It came to his apartment, but he wasn't living there and his friends hadn't paid it. I knew he had no power when his landline had an ongoing busy signal. By then, at the girlfriend's invitation, he had been living with his sons for five weeks.

But now the story has changed. The girlfriend told Anne, "I'm *letting* Tim stay with me because he has no power or phone."

Tim is working. He can get both electricity and telephone turned back on whenever the spirit moves. He hasn't bothered.

Friday, June 12, 2015

Tim got tired of the everlasting arguments with his girlfriend and asked me to come and pick him up. Unfortunately we had to go back to her bungalow twice: first for work clothes he had forgotten, and second with a box of freezies and a bucket of ice cream for the little boys.

The girlfriend told me, "They're both sick. We have no ice cream and no freezies," and she couldn't leave them to go shopping. I obliged.

It took ages to remove ourselves after the second stop; Tim and his girlfriend were talking and talking. I finally started the car, and unknowingly gave him the excuse he needed to hop in. He said it was difficult trying to figure out what she really wanted. She was ordering him to leave, and with the next sentence she was asking him to stay.

Sunday, June 21, 2015

I collected Tim at his girlfriend's bungalow, and we went out to his place of work to pick up his forgotten cell phone. When we were going back, he asked me to drop him off at a friend's apartment. He said he felt as if there was a ton of weight on his shoulders when he thought about seeing his girlfriend. She had been saying, "I hate you," and, "I wish you would leave." So he did; he has been absent for about a week.

He told me, "It's better for the boys if I'm not there. It isn't good for them to see us fighting all the time." He hates to see them cringing and pulling at their hands.

The girlfriend contacted me yesterday—I'm not sure why. She said Tim had been "missing for more than a week" (Kathleen and I had both seen him) and she had heard from a reliable source he was dealing drugs.

I was dying to say, "You buy *your* drugs from a dealer. What's the difference?" but I behaved myself.

Thursday, June 25, 2015

Tim was locked up briefly at the local police station. His girlfriend had him arrested for "harassment" and "uttering threats." He's out on his own recognizance. No other details, but at least I know where he is.

The girlfriend has managed to set up a much better reason for going through the legal system than just custody issues. I wonder who is coaching her.

Thursday, July 2, 2015

Kathleen and Tim had supper with me. Tim is in a total meltdown; anxious and distressed about not seeing his sons. I hope he'll be over the worst before long and able to get back to work. Alternatively, a new girlfriend might help.

Sunday, July 12, 2015

Tim goes to court on Wednesday. He asked if I could come with him.

I said, "Of course! It's already written on my calendar."

Since he feels the girlfriend's charges are out of line with his known behaviours, and since he hasn't yet had a meeting with his new lawyer, Tim plans to plead not guilty. Too bad. A plea of not guilty means a trial. With the courts so backed up, a trial will be months down the road and he will forget important details.

And what will happen in terms of visitation rights? The girlfriend is absolutely in control and Tim hasn't seen his sons for nearly a month. This is partly his own fault. He has been drinking (and probably using) to forget about his misfortunes instead of making changes for the benefit of his children.

However, he is more composed this week and has talked about going back to work.

Since charging Tim and setting up the no contact order, the girlfriend has been hanging around outside his apartment building. Tim lives in a second storey unit, and she parks on the driveway underneath his balcony for hours at a time. Is she trying to catch him committing a felony?

I said, "*That* could be termed harassment!"

Kathleen said, "No, Mom. That's stalking."

Something is really wrong here. Tim's girlfriend wasn't like this before—at least not around me. Her behaviours have become so odd. Tim says she smokes weed several times a day. According to scientific research, the psychoactive compound in marijuana may cause paranoia.

And then there's our Tim, born with a craving for alcohol and now drinking heavily to soothe his emotional pain.

James says, "Together those two make a whole parent." However, they are not together. I am feeling sick for the little boys and that doesn't help anybody or change anything.

Wednesday, July 15, 2015

A court appearance for Tim, which wasn't much more than showing up, meeting his new Legal Aid lawyer, Mark Thompson, and being put forward two weeks. The last lawyer was way better but she wasn't available this time.

Now Tim has to bring his new lawyer up to speed if he can. He is a wreck. He isn't working. Mostly he is drinking and dropping weight and crying. I will probably have to organize his appointment with his new lawyer. I will probably have to go with him to see his new lawyer.

Meanwhile, the girlfriend has involved me in an unusual police statement. I'll have to go down to the station and either have her story corrected or put in my own statement. She got it into her head Tim was going to kidnap her sons and spirit them off to the United States. How? He has no money, no car, and no American friends. I was supposed to be his accomplice. Where would I get the energy?

Friday, July 24, 2015

Tim phoned his lawyer to make the usual pre-trial appointment and had to leave a message.

The lawyer called back later and said, "We don't need to meet yet. Sit back and relax. Somebody will be bringing you papers."

Tim is in a tailspin, anxiously mulling this over, and phoning me regularly to see what I think it means. I think the girlfriend has invented another peculiar charge.

I will so appreciate my holiday in Alberta!! Can't wait to see Cricket and Clay and their children. We never plan anything touristy; it's just family fun. Life is so restful there. I can sit around drinking coffee and being a person of late middle age (or elderly, depending on your point of view) and my telephone doesn't ring.

Friday, August 7, 2015

We went to the lawyer.

Tim has changed his plea from not guilty on all charges to guilty for harassment. He goes back to court next Wednesday to set a date for sentencing. Probation has already been suggested by Crown.

The lawyer was surprised Crown had chosen harassment and was letting the rest of the girlfriend's charges go. He said harassment is "murky at best." But maybe the crown smelled a rat, considering some of the other absurd charges.

After next Wednesday, Tim can start fighting for mediation and permission to see the youngsters. Problem: he is now convinced his girlfriend is all-powerful and will forever have total control regarding his interactions with his sons.

Next week he is supposed to be connecting with his soon to be probation officer and setting up anger management and grief counseling because courses like those are impressive to judges.

Grief counseling was suggested by the girlfriend, who says Tim has never "got over" the deaths of his father and his brother, Alex. Of course not. We don't get over the death of a loved one: we learn to move on, is all.

Tim could use a lot of grief counseling because he's been missing his little boys, but the girlfriend would never be able to understand that. Or maybe I'm wrong. Maybe she understands perfectly and is out to destroy him.

Friday, August 14, 2015

The girlfriend, who had insisted on a no contact order, visited Tim's apartment building this morning. The elevator door opened for Tim to step on and there she was, inside. He quickly moved off down the hall as he is supposed to do; the door swished closed and the girlfriend went on up. He heard the elevator stop, as he expected it would, at her dealer's floor. She was using this dealer long before she and Tim became a twosome. And, apart from Tim and her dealer, she has no acquaintances living in the building.

What a blessing she didn't bring the children; she has taken them with her to the dealer often enough. They would have run out of the elevator and straight to Daddy.

Too bad Tim was denied the right to have a no contact order against her. With that on record, she wouldn't have been entitled to come to his place of residence.

Previously, both Tim and his girlfriend asked for no contact orders because, as each of them said, "I'm afraid of what might happen." She got the order. He didn't.

When I told the lawyer, he said, "Did you expect this to be fair? Tim is a guy."

We do not have a *justice* system. We have a legal system, and we have Corrections.

Thursday, September 3, 2015

My new computer glasses were supposed to be in this week but here it is Thursday and not a sign of them. Am I surprised?

The problem is not with the computer. It's my bifocals; they have stopped matching my vision. They are perfect for driving and reading and ordinary living, but they aren't correct anymore for extended computer work. On the right eye, I have to use the bottom lens. On the left eye, I have to use the top lens. There is no middle ground.

I'm glad the writing for *The Burning* is pretty much wrapped up. But then, writing is fun. Publishing isn't.

To organize the word mark, I had to connect with PayPal. To organize PayPal, I had to contact Mastercard. My credit card expired last December; it doesn't get used very often. They'll send a new card with a new number because they think the last one they sent might have been stolen. I never got it. Good thing I checked.

There will be an eight to ten day wait for the new card. Back to PayPal and go on hold. Back to Word Mark and go on hold. This is a long way outside my comfort zone.

Monday, October 11, 2015

Tim has moved from his half-decent apartment to something rather low end. I can't seem to get hold of any reason for this move, but apparently the girlfriend has been involved with his decision.

Sunday, October 17, 2015

We celebrated Thanksgiving in Victoria at Zan and Bedelia's place. Missing: Tim and family. Tim planned to join us but developed a "sore throat." My main beef with the girlfriend continues to be the way she uses her sons to punish their father—and so the rest of us. Zan's little ones couldn't understand why the twins didn't come.

Tuesday, November 3, 2015

Just had an extremely worrying discussion with Cricket. My granddaughter Kaitlyn has gone missing. She went to school today and attended first period but hasn't been seen since. This is *not* typical behaviour. There have been no family disruptions, and Kaitlyn carries a cell phone and keeps in touch with home.

The Calgary Police are being uncooperative, as Kaitlyn is seventeen and considered "an emerging adult." She's seventeen going on twelve with a history of mental health problems and a low IQ but nothing counts except chronological age.

Cricket phoned her sister in Ottawa, who works for the government and is in meetings this week about missing aboriginal women and girls. Our Kaitlyn is, at this moment, a missing aboriginal girl. Somebody from Ottawa called the Calgary Municipal Police, hit a blank wall, and promptly contacted Cricket and Clay, suggesting they use the RCMP instead.

Wednesday, November 4, 2015

I have a niece living in Calgary. Her partner and her partner's father and her partner's brother are all bus drivers, working for the City of Calgary. They already have Kaitlyn's photo posted in their buses and have asked their bus driving friends to do the same. They plan to query management today, asking if *all* Calgary buses can follow suit.

Thursday, November 5, 2015

It's 9:30 p.m. in Calgary. Cricket and Clay have just heard from the police. Kaitlyn is safe; her parents have nothing else to hold on to. They haven't seen her or spoken to her yet.

I will bet my last dollar there is a boyfriend involved in this, who has undercut Mom and Dad and talked Kaitlyn into leaving home. And she *loves* him!!! And he *understands* her!!!

Friday, November 6, 2015

Cricket and Clay have sent out a general email for all their friends and family. I have put a copy of it into Kaitlyn's box, along with her art projects and old photos and Christmas cards that I can't bear to throw away.

> This is a message to whomever Kaitlyn may reach out to.
>
> The past three days we have been rising and dropping on an emotional Ferris wheel because of poor decisions made by Kaitlyn. Now, even though we have been advocating for her, and fighting for her right to testing, and supporting her through her problems for years, at the age of seventeen she is legally entitled to do what she wants to do. Due to her rights no one can release information as to her whereabouts, other than she is safe.
>
> As her parents, we are asking everyone to join in this collaboratively. We are requesting, if she does reach out to anyone, she be informed that she is doing a great job on her own, with a reminder that she has a loving family to go to if she happens to need help. Please don't be the hero and "save" her.
>
> Kaitlyn needs to experience some life situations and now is the time. She has decided this. She is welcome to come home but we want to encourage her to do so on her own schedule. We won't let her end up on the streets; we are here for her. We will step in when needed.
>
> Because we know her best, we know what she will do. We are confident we have given her enough valuable life skills to not slip into the cracks. Many teens go through this stage, and we hope she will come out of it as a more mature adult.

We want the very best for her. So at this time please respect our request. We want everyone to know, with Kaitlyn's mental/emotional history, this is the best solution in our eyes. And if you do hear from her we would hope to be notified. (That's at your own discretion. No hurt feelings.) She has already phoned one family member, and seems to be OK. If she reaches out to you, please support her emotionally; she may need it.

If she contacts anyone with requests, please feel free to call us and see what we think. Sometimes in life what you hear from one person isn't necessarily the case.

Thanks everyone!

Clay and Cricket

I'm finding the "legally entitled to do what she wants at seventeen" ridiculous; it must be extremely frustrating for Cricket and Clay.

If Kaitlyn was living at home and her parents didn't take proper care of her, she would be apprehended and put into the care of the Ministry because she's still a minor. But when kids decide they're going to take off and do what they want, the parents are not at liberty to intervene. What a system!

Anyway, I'm very thankful she's safe.

And she is still going to school. What a cute little carbon copy of her Uncle Tim! He was also seventeen when he waved goodbye to me, rode down the street on his bicycle and from then on refused to come home. But he continued going to school for the first week or two.

Saturday, November 7, 2015

Cricket has heard from another mother, who hopes to remain anonymous. She said Kaitlyn is staying in her basement suite, and she shared several incidents. Some are worse than Cricket suspected; a few are better than she had hoped. The gaps are filled in. The new boyfriend now has a name and an address.

Cricket said, "It is super awesome she put her relationship with her own son in jeopardy to contact me, mom to mom. Now I have someone who will keep me posted, as long as Kaitlyn doesn't find out."

Kaitlyn has blocked her parents from her Facebook page. Chances are she discovered the letter they wrote, asking everybody not to empower her.

Sunday, November 8, 2015

Cricket wrote to tell me the drama is dying down. Kaitlyn contacted her aunt and uncle, Cricket's brother and sister, and they both gave her the same directive: "Go home!"

Cricket is feeling much better. She knew I supported her, but she thought her brother and sister might believe the lies Kaitlyn is spreading.

She said, "So this is good, even though I'm still worried and anxious." We all are. And we're all hoping for the best for Kaitlyn, and that she makes wise decisions.

Friday, November 20, 2015

We are getting started on plans for St. Nicholaas.

It was Peter who introduced our family to this saint and his feast day. Peter grew up in the Netherlands where St. Nicholaas Day was a fun festival, mostly for youngsters, and Christmas Day was a holy time of prayer and worship—a religious celebration.

I have no notion of what the Nederlanders eat on December 6, but *our* St. Nicholaas dinner has always been "stamppot met rook worst" (mashed potatoes mixed with sauerkraut and topped with slices of smoked pork sausage). This is an easily prepared traditional meal Peter's family ate at least once a week all winter. Our kids relish stamppot, but because assorted daughters-in-law and grandchildren find it a bit hard to take, Zan has been providing a large pot of nasi goring the last few years.

He says, "To augment the feast."

For dessert we always have pepernoten, boterkoek, and truffles. Most of those are already baked and buried in the freezer. And I have already gift-wrapped and tagged all the chocolate letters and put ribbons on candy canes. I even remembered to buy a box of oranges.

When our five were young, they put their shoes in front of the fireplace just before bedtime on December 5, with carrots tucked inside for St. Nicholaas's white horse. Black Pete, who travelled with St. Nicholaas and cared for his horse, needed the carrots. He came down the chimney with gifts to make a trade. The next morning the carrots were gone, and the children found toys and treasures in their shoes, along with an undecorated chocolate letter. St. Nicholaas didn't have time for elegant wrapping back in those hectic days.

Sunday, November 22, 2015

Another unhappy call from Cricket. Kaitlyn was taken to a medical center by her social worker. She "thought she might try to commit suicide."

The high school called to tell Cricket of this latest development. Kaitlyn had requested her mother *not* be contacted but legally, educational institutions must inform parents, as Kaitlyn understands perfectly well. This is about attention seeking; it's not about suicide.

Kaitlyn is the image of her birth father, my youngest son, Alex. Alex had been living in his very first boarding situation for four weeks before he "thought he might try to do it." His daughter lasted two weeks.

I really didn't need this.

Cricket is managing the whole situation far more capably than I ever did. She contacted the medical center at once and gave them Kaitlyn's mental health history. She recommended her daughter be admitted to the psychiatric wing, "Until she can get her crap together."

Tuesday, November 24, 2015

Last week Tim crashed his bike, resulting in a sharp pain in his side—another cracked rib? Following this accident, he stepped on his own earring stem and has ended up with an infected foot. He said he could manage the rib but the foot was throbbing.

I wanted to organize some medical help and pain relief for him yesterday, but Tim said, "I don't have the stamina to sit in a doctor's office so late in the afternoon."

He went to the walk-in clinic early today. The doctor ordered an antibiotic, and he has to go back if his foot keeps on hurting. I told him to come to my spare room for a couple of nights in case the pills make him sick. He usually has unpleasant reactions to antibiotics.

Thursday, November 26, 2015

Zan and Bedelia are in anticipation mode: two foster children, still toddlers, will be placed with them sometime during December. Their older two had the fun of phoning Oma and sharing this exciting news. I'm thrilled because Peter and I housed and cared for numerous fosters through the 1970s and 80s, and now it feels as if Zan and Bedelia are treading in our footsteps.

And two extra little ones just before Christmas…oh how this takes me back!

For Peter and me, all the extras were either babies or toddlers until two years after Zan was born. That fall we were asked to take on the unknown—a group of three older siblings. And, with the most perfect timing, we were also able to attend a Celebrations workshop through the Foster Parents Association.

From the FPA:

> Foster children endure unbelievably high levels of emotional stress, on top of having to deal with a

complete change of lifestyle and often a change of school. Our workshops are designed to keep foster parents mindful of this distress and to help ease the tension for our temporary children in the one area we can—daily living.

We learned a lot from all the workshops and the one on celebrations was especially good. I took pages of notes.

For these youngsters, with nothing the same as it had been at home, some of the most difficult moments were their birthday celebrations. Other important events (Halloween, Thanksgiving, Mother's Day, Easter) were also hard for them. But the families they had been dropped into already had their own ways of celebrating.

How to pull the two together?

Before a new foster child has a birthday, make sure a family member has one. Doesn't matter who; you can pull the baby's birth date up a month, or let Mom or Grandma cheat a little. The point is for the foster child to witness the way in which this family celebrates before his own special day comes along.

If the new child has materialized at your door just before, for example, St. Valentine's Day, try to find a craft or a cookie recipe that's new for everybody in the household. Along with the fun of working together, get the kids to talk about the occasion coming up and "what we always do." While being gently eased into your ways, the new child might give you a terrific idea to add to the whole family's enjoyment.

Our first group of siblings—three of them, all school age—came to us in mid November. There were no birthdays in the offing, but Christmas, a huge celebration in the eyes of the children, was already a central topic of conversation among my preschool crowd. Peter and I needed a way to celebrate Christmas before Christmas. I drew a blank, but Peter remembered the St. Nicholaas fun of his own childhood.

We have celebrated St. Nicholaas's Day ever since.

Monday, November 30, 2015

Our St. Nicholaas feast will have to be a bit later in the day than originally planned. Zan forgot he had signed up to help with the pancake breakfast at his church so our affair can't start until 2 p.m.

James and Elaine have a friend named Keith who is coming for St. Nicholaas. Hope my favourite candy shop can find me a chocolate 'K.' But we *will* have an extra 'L.' Tim's new girlfriend, Lynn, can't be with us. She is in custody over on the mainland at Alouette Correctional Centre for Women waiting for a trial.

The most crucial bit of my old kitchen machine (now known as a food processor) unexpectedly fell apart. It happened just as I was starting to grate eight cups of cheese. All that lot to do by hand! The grinding and mixing parts of my kitchen machine are unbroken, thank goodness, in view of Christmas baking and cranberry sauce.

Mediation has happened at last for Tim and his ex-girlfriend. Bit of a circus, really, held at a private home, on a weekend, and it went on for hours. They each had a lawyer present because the ex is officially "terrified" of Tim. Because Tim has FASD, he was allowed a support person. Then the ex insisted on a support person for herself, as well.

Tim said he had lost track of a lot of the discussion, but he knows the parents have a no contact order and the little boys will be having regular monitored visits with Daddy.

The supervision is because Tim's addictions are getting worse and worse, and not because any harm has ever happened to the twins. Even the contentious ex admitted her sons have never been hurt by their father.

We had hoped to see the twins and their mother at St. Nicholaas this year, and Tim offered to stay away, making it possible for them to come, but the ex doesn't want any contact with any of us. Too bad about what the children want.

Too bad about their Oma, also, who babysat them for two or three days each week ever since they were born. This has been a long, empty nine months.

Tuesday, December 1, 2015

My Pooch died a year ago. I had been considering getting another dog, especially since Tim started bringing his street friends to my house for meals, and now I've got one.

Last week Kathleen and I answered an ad, "Free to a good home," and unearthed Woocher. He is a cozy companion, wanting to be wherever I'm sitting or working, but seldom underfoot. He is big, about ninety pounds, and was well trained by his previous owners.

He stays on his own bed at night; doesn't run and play in the house; ignores any sirens going past; keeps off the furniture; doesn't put his paws on the counter; doesn't jump up on people; doesn't cower at little household noises. What more could anybody ask?

He likes raw carrot or raw broccoli or banana or my apple core for a treat.

He understands "Sit" and "Shake hands" and "Go on your bed" and is good about coming when requested. "Heel" is not part of his vocabulary.

We walked to the lake in rain and cold when nobody else was there. I let the dog run free. In seconds he was ten yards out, swimming alongside the shoreline and trying to catch sea gulls.

And Woocher has a friend. He and Kathleen's dog, Pooh, who is smaller and older, play in the wooded area behind my strata. They run through the trees, up and down the cliffs, and back and forth across the creek. Kathleen and I are thankful they get along so well and very pleased with the way they keep each other exercised.

Wednesday, December 2, 2015

Tim turned up, mad at the world. Lynn, his new girlfriend, had phoned him collect from Alouette Correctional in Maple Ridge to tell him how her trial went. He had said he would accept the charges, but then they were cut off because his wasn't an "approved account."

He told me he had made inquiries and all I had to do was prepay for a month. Then Lynn could stay in touch with him and I could take the cost out of his Christmas money.

It took forever to find out who and where to prepay and to organize with many different Corrections branches. (They're a big business; no wonder they want to keep this system going.) Tim wasn't about to leave until the whole undertaking was arranged in his favour.

When Corrections connected with my credit union here in town, the employees at the credit union thought I was being cheated by a fake company. They didn't trust the email address, and they asked me several security questions. Tim was totally frustrated. He wants instant gratification, always.

Prepaying is going to cost him a bundle and even now I'm not sure we got it right. There've been three emails from Canada Relink and I believe they should have gone to Lynn, not to me.

I sent Lynn a Christmas card to tell her Tim's phone has been activated. It isn't easy to find a Christmas card with a message suitable for someone in the slammer.

Sunday, December 6, 2015

St. Nicholaas Day.

James and Elaine came early because James wanted to use my oven to bake St. Nicholaas speculaas. Then, after dinner, he zipped around the block to my brother's place for a quick computer consultation. When he came back from helping Uncle Bruce, he fell asleep in the middle of the kids' movie. Elaine told us James had worked from 7 a.m. until 11 p.m. the day before. No wonder he ended up baking his cookies here!

I'm glad they all feel right at home. Following their movie, the youngsters pulled out the dress up trunk, and some of the adults started a board game. Bedelia boiled Norwex cloths in the kitchen.

Later on, Mary Grace made a pot of tea, and she and I sat on the top step and had an undisturbed few moments before she drove Tim home.

Mary Grace told me she had a conversation with Tim while they were still in the car, about how wrong she felt it was to not have his sons there. She asked if it had been hard for him when we talked about his children. He said it was fine; he was glad they had been remembered.

He added, "I'm pleased Mom has pictures of my boys spread all over her house."

But he won't hear one negative word regarding their mother.

When they got to the house where Tim is staying, this week, Mary Grace told him she would pray for him and for the little boys, but she thought she might have trouble praying for his ex.

He said, "You should; she needs it."

Friday, December 11, 2015

There are numerous little lifestyle changes here, thanks to my new dog. He needs at least three walks every day and I'm losing weight, which is splendid. Have to wash dishes immediately, nowadays, or I might forget and Woocher can easily reach the counters. Once he got used to me, he started sniffing for dirty dishes in the middle of the night. And I have to vacuum at least once daily. Rolls of long, soft black hair collect in all the corners.

Tuesday, December 15, 2015

Tim needed my help twice. This morning we went to the Ministry of Children and Family Development office *again* and he filled in the forms for visiting his little boys *again*. Fourth round: no action yet. I added a sentimental note; "Seeing Daddy for Christmas."

Later on, Tim had an appointment at his Band office. He had to get a new status card to replace the one he lost last month. It takes a whole afternoon to regroup a status card.

The alternative girlfriend, Lynn, who shares Tim's present addictions and who also got him started on heroin, will be coming out of Alouette in the near future. Lynn has a strong grandmother, a retired construction boss who rides a Harley Davidson. She stopped Tim on the street to have a little chat with him.

Lynn's grandmother and mother have accepted Lynn's desire to live with Tim, once she's on the outside. A warning has been issued: if Lynn's life falls apart, he will have her grandmother to deal with.

Tim is subdued and respectful—and a tad nervous.

Tuesday, December 22, 2015

Many years ago, to prevent divided loyalties, I started encouraging my lot to celebrate with their in-laws on Christmas Day.

We wanted to be together, of course, but it was much easier to assemble our large family on one of the restful days between Christmas and New Year's. We still do it that way; this year we are celebrating our family Christmas at noon on December 27. James and Elaine are hosting.

We had hoped Tim's sons could be part of the festivities, but their mother shot that down. Being an Oma out of contact with grandchildren is depressing.

Tim's new girlfriend is being released today, having resided at the women's correctional center for a month. Hope she will be drug free and able to cope with our Christmas family function.

And Kathleen is pouting because she can't bring her dog.

Friday, December 25, 2015

Christmas Day…

…and a typical gathering at my house. I had created a delicious meal; the expected guests were Kathleen, Tim, and Lynn. The lunch was supposed to be served at noon. Entertainment?—I hoped none.

Tim and his friend Sterling got here at 11:10 a.m., starving. Tim set the table and organized food with the speed of light. Woocher, who loves Tim and has taken a shine to Sterling, was continually underfoot until Sterling removed him to a corner of the kitchen for a private visit.

And where was Lynn? Tim said he and Lynn had shared a running battle yesterday "all over town," and hadn't finished fighting when they met Lynn's mother and her boyfriend this morning at the Seven-11. (The Seven-11 on Christmas Day?) Lynn had decided to stay with her mother. Tim thought the boyfriend was a decent sort, and very understanding.

Second lunch started when Kathleen showed up at 12:30 p.m., stressed and anxious.

Her apartment building has squirrel lovers who throw peanuts out of their windows, bird lovers who have feeders on their balconies, and now rats. Yesterday morning she found an expensive disaster in the cupboard where she keeps her bulk foods. The building manager told her he was too busy to deal with it and she should go and buy warfarin. When she found out warfarin is a poison she dissolved into floods of tears; she was positive the building manager wanted to kill Pooh.

Other residents helped her organize traps, but she couldn't sleep last night for three reasons:

1) She could hear the rat running in her cupboard.
2) Pooh was sick from something he ate at the park.
3) There was an attempted murder at her building, and the police officers were around most of the night.

I had promised to drive Tim home after his lunch because there was a lot of seasonal baking for him to take along. Very nice and all that but what he really wanted was his Christmas money. Long ago I stopped buying Christmas presents for my single, working kids. Instead, while they were young and unattached I did vast amounts of Christmas baking for them. Later, as I got older and their needs changed, the baking lessened and each family received a Christmas cheque.

Tim had already used $200 of his money setting up collect calls for Lynn while she was in Alouette. Another fifty dollars had been spent on two large cabinets left with me after the big church bazaar last September, and taking up space in my garage. Tim said he wanted them. We were halfway through December before he finally got them to his new boarding house thanks to a friend with a truck. This is the second place he has rented since he gave up his apartment.

Kathleen entertained herself by sorting through my jars of buttons. She needed two eyes for a stuffed rabbit she had made for one of Zan and Bedelia's new fosters. Sterling's entertainment was watching me fly up and down the stairs, finding boxes and organizing the baking for Tim and Kathleen to take home.

I had cookies for Sterling, as well. Tim's friends are all respectful, but Sterling is special; he's the one who lines up for a hug when it's time to leave.

Saturday, December 26, 2015

Kathleen and Pooh stayed with me on Christmas night, and will be here for tonight, as well. Uncle Bruce checked and reset the rat traps for her. I don't know how my daughter would manage without her uncle. She believes one caught rat will finish off her difficulties.

I have written to the city inspector and to the MLA's office asking for assistance to get the building manager moving. He *has* to deal with this problem; the whole apartment block is infested.

Sunday, December 27, 2015

Tim and I had fun organizing Christmas gifts and cards for the little boys. Delivery is tricky because he isn't permitted to go to their place of residence, and I'm not fond of going there. When the yellow car is parked beside the house the family is at home, but silent; the kids might move about and whisper, but nobody comes to the door. If they are not at home, bags left hanging on the doorknob are close to the main road and too easy to see from the sidewalk.

The compromise: I deposited two extra-large gift bags full of presents at the other grandparents' home on December 23, and asked them to make sure the contents got to the twins.

The other grandmother told me there has been a further separation in her family. Her son and his wife have split up, so now we are *both* being deprived of our grandchildren.

Amazing what fellow feeling can do.

Tim's ex-girlfriend left a phone message on Christmas Day. Her mother had talked to her; did I want to come to her parents' place for coffee on Sunday and see the twins?

I went this afternoon and it was a slightly strained but otherwise delightful experience. The ex was there; also her mother and father. I was carefully supervised. They had held back the little boys' gifts from Daddy and me and Aunty Kathleen until I got there. It was fun watching the kids open parcels and reading their cards to them.

Twin One managed to catch me alone in the hallway and whispered, "I wish I could talk to my Daddy."

I almost felt guilty, going to see Tim's sons without Tim. However, he never was allowed to attend any parties or social gatherings with his girlfriend's extended family. The children went to Grandma and Grandpa with Mommy; Daddy always had to stay behind.

Monday, December 28, 2015

Kathleen and I (but not Tim or Lynn) started off to Victoria for our family Christmas dinner but we turned back before we reached Malahat Mountain. The snow was getting deeper and deeper, and I was getting more and more nervous driving through it.

Kathleen didn't mind missing the dinner: she has one focus at this moment— rats. She and Pooh are still staying with me.

She says, "Until dude is gone."

I say, "Until the rat holes are filled with steel wool."

Her next chore is buying steel wool so Uncle Bruce can help stuff the holes. Kathleen is terrified at the thought of going into her apartment and is doing her best to offload this whole problem. I have to keep on insisting re: the next move.

Woocher hasn't been hearing properly; we went to his vet. He has a juicy ear infection, now cleaned up and being healed with an expensive antibiotic. I get to squirt it into his bad ear twice a day. No problem: he cooperates.

The vet remembered me from Pooch's death a year ago. Her first comment: "I'm glad to see you under happier circumstances."

I told her about Kathleen's rats and the manager's suggestion regarding poison. No doubt the local vets will be overwhelmed with poisoned dogs and cats, considering the numerous citizens with mental health problems and addictions living in Kathleen's big apartment building, who are now putting out rat poison.

Monday, December 29, 2015

Bruce and Alana both helped with the rat proofing of Kathleen's apartment. Bruce said they did it for me, as much as for their niece.

Kathleen and Pooh stayed here for four nights, avoiding the rats. Woocher and I sent them on their way this morning, after breakfast and a walk. Kathleen is anxious about going home and suggested extending her stay, but her home support housekeeper comes on Tuesdays. She certainly does need help to tidy and reorganize her belongings. And she wants to get all her bulk food into plastic and metal containers.

Wednesday, December 30, 2015

Earthquake!!

I felt it; one little wiggle and done. Not the long, rumbly kind you can hear coming and feel in waves.

Thursday, December 31, 2015

Kathleen is back. Fortunately, I hadn't changed the guest room sheets. Must have unconsciously anticipated more trouble.

She said, "The rats were quiet until the earthquake. Then they began running through the walls and one started rattling my heater."

Knowing it was in the bedroom, she stayed awake in the living room for the whole night. Then Donald, her neighbour, came over, and found steel wool pulled out of the hole and onto the floor of her unit.

Kathleen said, "When the earthquake scared him, Dude tried to scratch his way back into the divider. Donald heard the action."

Her neighbour set traps in the bedroom and stuffed the last of the steel wool into the hole.

Kathleen wants both of us to work at her apartment tomorrow. I reminded her of how much I nag for the removal of everything not in use or broken, even if it has Walt Disney's Winnie the Pooh on it. But Kathleen said she badly needs help and direction and she'll try not to get mad at me.

2016

Wednesday, January 13, 2016

Kathleen and Pooh have been living with Woocher and me for nearly two weeks. She won't stay in her own apartment alone.

Whatever needs to be done for my household, Kathleen wants to join me while I do it. I'm having to let most of my activities wait, apart from grocery shopping, since Tim and his friends still eat here frequently.

Hoping to send her home soon, I've got us on a tight schedule and we are both putting as much energy and enthusiasm as possible into her muddle.

We have caught three rats already. Uncle Bruce is marvellous about removing the bodies and resetting the traps.

Since December 26, I've made Kathleen go through every box, every drawer, every shelf, and every cupboard, first in her bedroom and then in the living room. We have chucked out innumerable bags of garbage and even personal effects that aren't garbage if a rat has been on them.

We have started the kitchen.

Everywhere, there were folded pants Kathleen had plans to turn into shorts "someday."

I said, "When? There are ten pairs, so far."

She didn't believe me; a search was organized. Seventeen pairs. We conveyed the whole box to my spare room, and the intervals she thought would be for resting have gone into trying on pants and making decisions and cutting and hemming.

Last week the building manager told my daughter there were no wild rats in her apartment. What she was hearing and seeing was a tame, pet rat: an escapee from one of the units. He said if Kathleen had a problem with that, she could leave. She promptly decided he was evicting her and started to panic.

Tuesday, January 19, 2016

We are seeing the end of the rat problem in Kathleen's apartment, although not in the building as a whole.

The traps haven't been sprung for four days; we washed them and put them away. Carpets are being steam cleaned, with much shifting of furniture and boxes. We are getting down to the dust on the kitchen shelves. Organization of everything still in the apartment looms—and will be temporary, as Kathleen can't resist a "bargain," even a bargain she doesn't need and will never use.

Basically, we are doing seven years of housekeeping in one month and it's heavy going.

Most important—she now feels safe in her own home.

The Ministry of Children and Family Development has contacted Tim. Because he was originally told monitored parenting of his sons had to be arranged through the Ministry, we have been haunting their office, begging for a worker and filling in forms in triplicate.

Now they're telling him he didn't need to go through anybody; his visits with the children are set up and have been for three months, and where is he?

Tuesday, February 9, 2016

Yesterday was Family Day. To celebrate, James and Elaine arranged a relaxed, congenial afternoon with me. James produced a little gadget for the interior of my monitor. I'll be able to play DVDs on the computer! Wahoo!!

Invariably there are chores waiting for James, poor chap. Today I asked him to check my office workspace. Last week, the man from

Shaw Cable came by to make some telephone changes and I wanted to be sure he had put my office back together properly. Various electronic devices worked well, but they were in different places and they didn't look the same.

We had a lovely supper at Good Neighbour.

There are many ways to 'celebrate' Family Day.

My doorbell rang at 7:30 this morning and there was Tim, throwing up on my lawn. For breakfast, he ate two buns with cheese, a baking powder biscuit with cheese, a banana, and four cans of Coke. He left with two more biscuits and two more Cokes.

Then he phoned twice while James and Elaine were here. The first call was an accidental pocket dial with lots of background music and swearing but nobody conversing.

The second call was to tell me he and Lynn had to leave their boarding house because the landlord was going nuts. He had attacked them with his fists, and was blaming them for every single one of his problems. They knew he had a gun upstairs and that he had shot at other tenants.

I said, twice, "What are you going to do?" but Tim couldn't move beyond the landlord who was "going nuts."

I suggested, "Maybe you need to ask Lynn's mother to come and get her out of there … " and Tim hung up. Haven't heard any news since.

Monday, February 15, 2016

Lynn and Tim have split up. It might last. Tim came by at suppertime and told me, "Lynn has moved in with an old man who came into money."

About twelve others are there too. All of a sudden the old man has lots of friends, all using.

Tim has told Lynn he doesn't want to see her again until she "comes back from rehab." Hope he can stick to this plan.

Monday, February 22, 2016

This morning a young RCMP officer escorted Tim to my door and told me the landlord had thumped my son on the top of his head with a hammer.

Tim added, "For no reason."

He wouldn't go to a doctor. He slept for a while, and then went out to meet Sterling, who had managed to liberate Tim's bike through the back fence of the boarding house while the officers were keeping the landlord busy at the front. At suppertime Tim showed up to have a wash and change his clothes but he didn't stay. Nor did he say where he was going to spend the night.

Tuesday, February 23, 2016

Tim and I, and a friend with her truck, and a different officer, went to Tim's ex-residence and we got his clothes, Lynn's clothes, their electronics and other odds and ends. He left behind his bed, his TV, a table, an easy chair, and the two enormous cabinets from my garage. He really wanted those cabinets, and they were in my garage for months, and my car had to live outside well into the winter to accommodate them, and now look.

Today, since noon, Tim has been sleeping upstairs, either because of the head injury or because of being out on the prowl all night, or both. I think he plans to stay here tonight. He said he was moving in "with Bear and those guys," but the ex-landlord has his rent for March.

Or maybe not? Maybe missing money was the reason he used his hammer on Tim's head.

Wednesday, February 24, 2016

Tim went with me to the hospital. He was willing to go because he was having a sick stomach, dizziness, and a throbbing earache. And I'm thankful for these new symptoms as he was planning to "get even" with the character who hammered him.

The medical personnel did a scan. Tim has a concussion. He is supposed to rest for a week and take painkillers as needed. To rest, he dismantled his bicycle and painted it. The pieces are hanging on strings around my living room, getting dry.

Thursday, February 25, 2016

I've decided to get involved with sorting out Tim's regulated parenting time since nothing has happened for six months. This is not officially my business and plenty of people have frowned upon my involvement. But nobody will move on it if I don't.

The mediation paperwork, unavailable until recently, told us a new supervisor was supposed to be arranging everything. Tim asked me to telephone him.

The new supervisor said he was ready, anytime, and the delay was with Tim.

I said I had talked to Tim's lawyer and everything was in order, and why wasn't the supervisor getting things started?

The supervisor said Tim's lawyer had to give the ex's lawyer the go-ahead, and he hadn't yet, so visits were on hold.

I phoned Tim's lawyer and told him to GET ON WITH IT!!!

He said he would.

Then I got hold of *my* lawyer and talked to her about getting a new legal advisor for Tim.

Sunday, February 28, 2016

Tim is a different man from the sick, sullen disaster we dealt with a week ago. He is eating normally, sleeping at night, not using as far as I know, keeping up with his commitments, and reconnecting with family and friends. Stability, and hope, and a concussion have made such a difference!

Lynn went missing, thank God, and Tim has been supporting her mother.

Tim's possessions (the ones not left behind at his boarding house) are here and he is here often: sometimes for meals; sometimes for sleep. We get along pretty well because I'm always pleased to see him, have very few expectations, and try to be accommodating. If only his ex-girlfriend could have understood this is the best way to manage my son. She always said she had three children but then she expected adult behaviour.

Likely Tim will stay with me until his next rent money comes along. He waffles between living alone and shared housing. He hates being by himself but sharing means roommates similar to Lynn.

I am a firm believer in supervised housing, organized either through the courts or through probation but it'll never happen in my lifetime.

We have talked to the extremely youthful probation officer who will be doing the pre-sentencing report. Tim and I both liked him.

Tim said, "He looks like a little kid, but I think he has all his ducks in a row."

The Legal Aid lawyer continues to be a twit, but sadly, we are stuck with him.

Wednesday, March 2, 2016
James and Elaine have invited me to go to Vancouver with them next week. Dog is nicely set up: Tim isn't. I don't want to leave him in my house on his own because it would finish with Lynn or somebody worse staying here, too. He wouldn't intend for anything to happen, but somehow …

At the moment, we will either have to take Tim with us to Vancouver or I will have to cancel. However, many changes can occur in a week.

Meanwhile, Tim and I are both sick. I've got a bad cold—not a surprise after a day spent at Zan and Bedelia's with grandchildren. Tim bumped his head on the corner of my cupboard door, in exactly the same spot the hammer hit, and his ear has started to hurt again. Will try to get him back to his doctor; that ear isn't cooperating.

I wrote a careful letter to the other lawyer (the one the ex-girlfriend uses) and he sent back a friendly reply. Tim's visits with his kids might get off the ground at last. At the moment, he is too sick to care.

Saturday, March 5, 2016

When I woke up this morning, the kitchen door was unlocked. A quick trip upstairs—Tim's bed was empty.

At 9:30 a.m. he sent me an email. He had gone for an early bike ride and had met Mike and Bear. He was at Bear's suite and planning to come back to me for lunch. He had remembered to take his new antibiotic.

His next contact was another email at 11:30 p.m. apparently to say good night. He thought he might see me in the morning, and finished with, "Taken pills, everything good."

Tuesday, March 8, 2016

Back to the clinic this morning. The doctor was satisfied with Tim's ear, and he was proud of himself for taking his tablets properly. Hope he can keep it up; there's just a few left.

Woocher had to go back to the vet—his sticky rash has started again, worse than ever. He didn't have this problem when I got him.

The vet shaved him, leaving two bare spots, and I have to wash those with an antiseptic liquid soap. Otherwise, he has to stay dry. No swimming.

And now we are working on allergies. Back to the expensive fish and pulse crumble he was on when he came to live with me, rash free. No treats, no snacks, nothing but dry dog food and sweet potatoes. I stuff his new antibiotic into a bit of sweet potato; he gulps it down. No poultry. No eggs. No red meats. No grains. No dairy. He'll have to stay on boring dog food until the rash doesn't come back. Two months? ... three? At some point we'll be able to start with slow, careful additions. Vegetables and fruits first (Woocher loves every sort of fruit except oranges) and maybe a second protein.

He has to be gluten free from here on in. A gluten free dog! I can't believe I've come to this.

Wednesday, March 9, 2016
Tim has sent another email about another apartment. I'm glad he has decided to live with the guys instead of with me, but I've started a new file for everything connected with his living arrangements. His housing seems to be so precarious.

> Morning mom, I will be moving here to Bear's rent is split 3 ways, him and me and Mike. each of us pay 350$ / month, split hydro. So if u want to hook the phone up here that would be much appreciated. I told them about my ex-landlord taking this months rent. Still figuring out things. Feeling good about this.

I've met Bear—he's uncommunicative but polite. Mike is easier; friendly and outgoing. Both of them will be more suitable roommates than Lynn. Mike and Tim have shared space in the past and have remained on congenial terms.

Monday, March 14, 2016
After the concussion, Tim's ear bled; later it got infected. The infection has started again, and he is back with me. He says he wants to stay until his ear has improved; the pain must be distressing.

We went to the walk-in clinic early. Luckily, Tim got the same doctor as before. She had started him off on a general antibiotic, but the culture came back with what Tim described as negative news. She has put him onto a much stronger medication based on the new lab work. He is feeling very ill and mostly sleeping.

Thursday, March 17, 2016

Although he's not completely fit, Tim has moved to his new rental suite. He said he loved his mother, but he was going stir crazy.

The twins' needs are being badly neglected. The organization of a little bit of parenting time for Daddy is still not happening, due to an unusually poor choice of supervisor. The fellow has yet to shift his butt on the children's behalf.

But legal efforts are not moving towards either getting a new supervisor or meeting the little boys' needs. Instead, they are setting up another mediation and worrying about the date. If the purpose of this next mediation is to see how the visits went, then it makes sense to have it quickly because there haven't been any visits, and obviously the other side has messed up.

This is my opinion, not Tim's. He told me I had to be civil no matter what. But I get to be the mom. Mothers and grandmothers take strong positions. And besides, I have become old and sour in the service.

And a request from the extremely youthful probation officer. He wants me to meet with him next week, for my part of the pre-sentencing report. Haven't had to be involved with one of those since Tim was in his twenties.

The courts ask the probation officers to write these reports to help them decide what to do with the offender. Counseling? Community service? Jail? When Tim was young, they wanted opinions from his parents regarding our relationship with our son, and his maturity, character, behaviour, and ability to make amends. I tried to be helpful: Peter flatly refused to be involved in any way.

Later, in court, everything I had said to the PO came out, right in front of Tim. I hate pre-sentencing reports!

Friday, March 18, 2016

There's a cataract growing on my bad eye. The ophthalmologist said most cataracts grow exceedingly slowly; with removal, there are noticeable changes in vision and new glasses are necessary. But mine is a fast-growing cataract, and when it is corrected my vision won't have changed.

It hasn't bothered me much, but I've been aware of a slight opaqueness for a while, primarily when going around our new roundabouts. Now I'm starting to have a noticeable blur on the left. Although the doctor hasn't put any limits on my driving, I have decided it would be a sensible choice to only drive in my home area until after the surgery.

My first eye operations were in 1954 and 1956. I was a little kid, but I was put into Royal Jubilee's ophthalmic unit with all the old ladies, rather than the children's ward. I can still remember the aftermath of those old style cataract surgeries. Two weeks as motionless as possible with both eyes bandaged, and with, at first, sandbags on both sides of the head to prevent the slightest movement. Then two more weeks, still in hospital, still with one eye bandaged and using a wheelchair. No reading or fine work for six months.

Nowadays cataract surgery takes about ten minutes. You walk out of the operating room. Immediately following the surgery you can read and watch TV, and after a checkup the next morning you are permitted to drive.

Saturday, March 19, 2016

Sterling has died. An overdose. He was living at Tim's old boarding house and he wasn't found for twenty-four hours. I'm so thankful the officers removed Tim from there after the hammer incident. But he said if he had been there Sterling wouldn't have died, and this is likely true. My son does keep an eye on his friends.

Police officers are often parked in front of that building—maybe this incident will close it down.

I met Lynn at the library last week when I was searching for Tim. Lynn sent me on to the food bank; the food bank sent me on to the doctor's office, and there was Tim, exactly where he was supposed to be. He had forgotten his plan to meet me at the library so we could both go to the follow up appointment with his doctor. No problem. I'm glad he felt confident enough to forget about me and go alone.

Wednesday, March 23, 2016

Haven't had a moment to write, the last few days, so this is catch up time.

Tim's new housing has gone by the wayside. Bear's carpet surfer got arrested for breaking into mailboxes and stealing mail. Bear's landlord wasn't in favour of police cars parked in front of his building for the duration; he ousted the whole group.

There are other friends Tim could stay with, or he could try to get a place in his sister Kathleen's apartment building and live with the rats. Unfortunately this is Welfare Wednesday, the unofficial first day of the month for the hard to house, and everything available will have been snapped up on March 1.

Tim's bank card was stolen, along with his status card, and BCID, when he left the boarding house. He had to regroup with his bank and he felt they were being "mega uncooperative" at Toronto Dominion. He was sent to the welfare office "Twice!" for signing and stamping. Then, with the paperwork finally in order to access his own account, he realized the government hadn't done his automatic deposit for Disability Wednesday. Tim might have forgotten to do the monthly application.

He told me this in the heck of a temper and didn't listen for long enough to discover, in case he happened to want it for himself, that his sister is using my extra bed.

Kathleen called, whooping and howling because she saw a rat!! She and her dog needed to come to me for a few nights.

This is impossible. Her home has to be rat free—she lived with me all through January while she and I and her loving family fought the Battle of the Beast.

We went through Kathleen's apartment and found no indication of a rat being housed. Kathleen says, since the whole building is infested, it must have come in from the passage when she came home.

She bought the foam the building manager has not authorized for use, and Uncle Bruce sprayed it on top of all the steel wool already there. And he filled a tiny hole Kathleen had discovered under the fridge. He also set two traps. Hopefully, if there is another rat, it will be caught with speed and this episode will be finished. Kathleen will be staying with me until either the rat is caught or the cheese dries up.

Tim must have gotten hold of his money—he has dropped off the face of the earth.

Sunday, March 27, 2016

The weatherman had said hail but we didn't get any. I got thundercloud Tim instead.

He had been at the church breakfast. Kathleen told me he went downstairs, following mass, and had a big helping of pancakes and sausage; then he waited for me in the foyer. But I didn't stay for the breakfast; I went home and enjoyed an extended walk with Woocher.

When we got back, there was Tim at my door, grumpy, dirty, and exhausted, although not hungry. Following a shower and a rest, he was much more open and sociable. He is doing a lot of physical labour down on the river, with a group of men who are cleaning up last year's homeless campsite and getting it ready for this year. He carried in his wet laundry, covered with mud and sand, and left it on the floor in front of my washing machine.

We had a chat about rent money. Tim is on rent direct: if he doesn't use it, he loses it. But he won't have an address if he is tenting on the river. No address means no rent money will be included in his disability pension. He wants to give the authorities my address. Then his rent money will come to my mailbox, and I can pass it on to him.

Why not? He is storing belongings here and eating with me and using my supplies and sleeping upstairs as the spirit moves. I'm paying for his razor blades, Q-tips, lighters, cigarettes, candles, matches, batteries, and tarps, not to mention pop, and ice cream treats. I'm providing showers and doing his laundry. He might as well be living here!

But I doubt if he will be able to get his financial situation organized while he is using heroin.

Thursday, March 31, 2016

Tim heard from the mediator, in person. A new date has been set for the second meeting—April 25. He had been expecting another endless wait, as the earlier "checkup" meeting was cancelled. Since there were no interactions between father and sons for six months there was nothing to check up on.

At this time, the ex-girlfriend won't assent to the little boys being with their daddy, even with outside supervision, in spite of signing to say she would do so. I find this very strange. Although her behaviours aren't FASD related, there are times when she doesn't have a good grasp of her own realities. It's almost as if she is trying to damage *herself* as much as she tries to undermine Tim.

Don't know which is more complicated to deal with: Tim's brain damage or whatever is wrong with the ex. Paranoia? Borderline psychosis? Personality disorder? We used to be friends but now I can't understand her at all.

As Oma, I have been campaigning for the twins' right to see their father. Maybe one of my letters caught the eye of a person with influence. But Tim suspects his ex has been dragging her heels so she can get in front of a judge and share the years of dirt she has collected and tabulated against him. In mediation, the past is past, and not to be discussed.

Either way, there might be some action at last.

Wednesday, April 6, 2016

While getting ready to see the eye surgeon, I broke my glasses. Not across the nose as happened last year; this was an arm snapped off. Frustration! But at least the optometrist's office is close to my ophthalmologist. I went to them before my 9:15 a.m. appointment and found they don't open for business until 9:30. More frustration!

But when I finally got back down there, the marvellous employees in the optometrist's office had saved the arms of my last pair of broken glasses, and they fit this pair perfectly! *And* they match. So much frustration wasted.

My eye surgery will be in four to six months. The doctor said the cataract is not bad, yet, but the fast-growing ones are quite noticeable for the person living with them.

He asked if I had thought about getting my wonky eye corrected.

I said, "Of course! Wouldn't you? But I've been told there is no possibility of adjustment."

He thinks there might be something new in laser surgery, and he's sending me to the leading children's eye surgeon in Victoria for a consultation. He said the consultation could happen before the cataract surgery. Not. Specialists are booking at least a year in advance.

Thursday, April 7, 2016

Tim and Lynn showed up at 2 p.m. hoping for a late lunch.

Lynn has one front tooth left (at twenty-three!) thanks to cocaine, and she has open sores all over herself, thanks to heroin.

I have learned too much.

During their conversation I got hold of Tim's *real* housing problem. Previously aided and abetted by his ex-girlfriend, who is constantly searching out new sources of income, my son managed to cancel his rent direct. Now the rent portion of his disability pension is being shifted from his bank account to his pocket each month. It doesn't ever go to rent. That's why he has so much money for drugs and no place to live.

Right back where we started, more than twenty years ago.

No wonder he is having all these housing problems. No wonder the landlord at the boarding house hit him with a hammer. The man has guns, too. Tim got lucky.

He told me he is presently sharing space with Carmen and her boyfriend. They have one bedroom, and my son sleeping on their living room couch, plus a carpet surfer who comes and goes and pays nothing. With Tim's $400 a month they expect to be able to afford a two bedroom apartment next month.

They will never get the $400 unless they all go to the bank, shoulder to shoulder, early on Welfare Wednesday.

They are living at what used to be the Cozy Corner. Tim has been evicted from Cozy Corner often in the past, but now it has been renamed The Cedars and is under new management. This building is at least one step above Rat Heaven where Kathleen lives; they are limited to cockroaches at The Cedars. Lynn spent a night or two with Carmen last year—she thinks Tim is lucky to be going there. She told him it was the best of his possible housing leads.

After they left, I phoned the Ministry of Social Development trying to find out what happened to Tim's rent direct. It had been officially red flagged and, I thought, written in stone. They had no idea; they could only offer a lot of sympathy and what's the use of that?

"All you can do is go to the local office and try to get it changed back."

But I already know the local crowd won't move forward with me unless Tim signs the Consent to Disclosure. And I already know he won't sign.

Saturday, April 9, 2016

Tim came in this morning muttering about breakfast and with two major issues. He had forgotten the bank wouldn't let him access his account unless he had ID. He could get proof of ID Monday to Friday, but this was Saturday. He was angry; he needed his money.

But much worse: he had left a stack of clothes at Mike's hovel, and Mike had sold Tim's hockey jerseys for drug money, and he thought Mike was his friend. He was crying about the lost jerseys as well as being mad.

I said, unkindly, "This wouldn't have happened if you had rent direct. You would have had a safe spot for your possessions and a key to lock the door."

Tim started to yell, and I learned some new swear words.

He was planning to kill Mike.

He was going out to rob a bank.

Who cared if he went to jail; he wasn't seeing his boys anyway.

And he was busy making plans to take the boarding house landlord to court.

And his rent money belonged to *him*; it was *his* money. I always thought rent money was for paying rent. We live and learn.

Tim stalked around and came close to leaving, but his breakfast was waiting for him. He went back and sat down. And ate. I wouldn't have been able to.

Surprisingly, I stayed unruffled while he emoted. It is so important (and so challenging) to *not* take verbal abuse personally when it comes from individuals who are struggling with an FASD.

Turned out Tim needed me to "lend" him $225 for Carmen. "That's all she wants until payday."

Then, when he finally had his ID organized, and could get at his disability money, I would be paid back.

He promised, "We will go to my bank together on Monday."

I decided to let him have the $225 for Carmen, although getting it back is doubtful. We went up to The Cedars, and I put the money into Carmen's hand and made her sign for it. Tim and Carmen both got a kick out of that—it was businesslike and gave them an adult feeling.

Later, I phoned Carmen's mother. We are acquainted; she and her daughter came to Alex's funeral. My Tim and her Carmen share a long history—same age, same town, same schooling, same street friends, both adopted, both stumbling through life with an FASD. It was a pleasure to talk to another mother who gets it.

Carmen's mother will talk to Carmen about Tim's money; she will "suggest" her daughter insists on regular trips to the bank with Tim. Carmen is exceptionally wise when it comes to money *owed* her, but she has been kicked out of every rental place in town, even Rat Heaven, for not paying her monthly fees. The Cedars is her last hope.

Her mother and I laughed about the planned two bedroom apartment—a delightful daydream. Anyway, the $225 will feed them for the next two weeks, and they might possibly manage another month following Welfare Wednesday. Carmen's mother has my number and she will stay involved. I will keep on talking about rent direct and will keep on not being heard.

But changes have to happen because I need my garage, not to mention my peace of mind. Two choices for Tim: he can move his stuff either upstairs to the spare bedroom or down into my crawl space, or else he has to get his possessions out of here, even if it means putting them into a storage unit.

Monday, April 11, 2016
Woocher and I went to the off leash river park. He isn't supposed to swim until his latest antibiotic is finished (ninety-nine dollars because of *another* skin infection) and he was obedient about staying out of the water. But he found the one rotten fish in the whole park, left under the bank after last winter's flooding, and he rolled in it.

I called the vet; Woocher *had* to have a bath.

The vet said, "Go ahead, but he will need to be blow-dried afterwards. And first you had better come in for a bottle of medicated shampoo." Another eighteen dollars.

The dog wouldn't go near the bathtub or the shower. I tied him to the crab apple tree outside my door and used the hose. Drying took forever, with soft black hair spread from hell to breakfast. And he continued to stink ferociously.

We walked down to the lake where dogs must be leashed but there was nobody else there. I sent him off to swim behind the ducks. After his swim the stink was much less; my eyes weren't burning anymore.

Back home, we had another session with the blow drier. My washing machine has been going full blast: dog towels, and blankets from the car, and jackets, and two changes of clothes.

Tuesday, April 12, 2016

A distress call from Carmen.

Tim had a bad fall at the community center. He crashed down their concrete stairs, did a face plant, and monkey wrenched his knee. Carmen said he couldn't get to the bank—he can hardly walk. Would I bring something for the pain? Tim thought there were pain capsules left from when his ear was bad. And could I stop on the way and buy him a pack of cigarettes?

His face is scraped and his eye is bruised. He said he felt the knee twist and that made him fall. He will phone me if he decides it needs a doctor.

Friday, April 15, 2016

Just when I thought there might be several improvements around here such as firming up rent direct or getting my garage back, Tim, as his grandma used to say, "upped the ante."

He broke his collarbone. For the fifth time.

How it happened is a mystery. Lynn and Tim said, "a fall," but with significant glances at one another. After the damage had been done they walked for an hour before they asked Kathleen to drive them to Emergency. They couldn't reach me.

Tim said, "I was trying to plan a way of getting help without going to the hospital."

Kathleen phoned me from Emergency. She said Tim was waiting

for pain relief, x-rays, and a diagnosis. Lynn had already vanished with Tim's backpack. Kathleen couldn't stay much longer but she didn't want to leave her brother by himself. I was in the middle of a battle with income tax forms but promised to relieve Kathleen in less than thirty minutes.

I found Tim exasperated. He already knew the bone had snapped; he wanted a clavicle brace, a pill for pain, and to get out of there. But at Emergency they do it their way.

When Tim was finally approved to go, they told him: "Wear the brace...Ice...A reclining chair...Physio...Medication for pain...Don't ride your bike...See your family doctor in a week."

He was willing to wear the brace, take the pills, and maybe see his doctor.

He went back to Carmen's apartment for the first night. No food, no ice, no recliner, and worst of all no cigarettes, but Lynn reappeared and helped him change and wash.

I caught a horrifying glimpse of the inside of the apartment while dropping off a bag of basic groceries.

Tim walked down to my house, nearly two miles, for the second night. At 9 p.m. when I came home from playing Mahjong, there he was, sitting on the lawn in the dark. He said he had been there since 7:30.

I will never forget Tim's first broken collarbone.

It was almost suppertime, and I was standing on the back porch, ringing our dinner bell when there was an unusual noise—a small but heavy thud. I walked around the corner to see what had happened. Five year old Tim was sitting on the grass under a tree.

I said, "Did you fall out of the tree?"

Tim said, "No," and, foolishly, I believed him.

He was quiet all evening. But since he was the most silent member of a large, loud family we didn't notice anything unusual until the next morning. He was unable to get out of bed; he couldn't lift his shoulders from the pillow.

Another fall from a different, taller tree caused Tim's second fractured collarbone.

We were on a community well; a mid summer water meeting had been convened. Parents were discussing various watering issues and their children were outside, playing and climbing. Tim, now almost seven, was nearing the top of a tree, with James, almost ten, close behind him and monitoring his climb, when Tim's branch broke. He started a slow drop through the other branches, falling past James, who grabbed for him and missed. He got caught on branch after branch; the interrupted fall meant a much lighter landing.

Peter stayed with Kathleen, Zan, and Alex. I borrowed blankets, wrapped them around Tim and James, and drove to Emergency. Tim, with tears pouring down his cheeks, was moaning softly and breathing in short, sharp gasps; James, white-faced and silent, was shaking uncontrollably.

The doctor took care of James first. "Shock," he said, and for Tim, "He has broken his collarbone and snapped a rib, but it could easily have been his neck."

Tim recovered quickly, but this accident gave James nightmares for months.

About ten days after his third collarbone break, Tim went for a drive with Alex, who had recently acquired his driver's license. Alex rear ended another teenage driver who had deliberately braked right in front of him. The recently repaired collarbone got a severe jolt and Tim said he heard it crack. That was break number four. Alex wasn't found to be at fault; the other driver's insurance had to pay.

Tuesday, April 19, 2016

Family Court was postponed. *Again*. Last month the pre sentencing report from the probation officer was "too late" and Tim's lawyer, Mark Thompson, said he hadn't had time to read it. Today Mr. Thompson said he couldn't imagine what had happened, but the pre sentencing report had gone missing and he hadn't read it. The officious court secretary handed a copy to the judge but she said, "Don't bother. Mr. Thompson hasn't seen it. We can't go on."

So the ex-girlfriend's charges are still waiting.

Tim and I are supposed to go and have a little chat with Mr. Thompson who was smart enough to catch Tim in the other corridor and avoid me.

Family members of the ex were in the courtroom. I recognized a sister and an aunt. They wasted a trip. So did we. I get myself psyched up and Tim calmed down, and all for nothing.

Hearing "our marvellous Canadian justice system" extolled would make me laugh if it wasn't so infuriating. Delay after delay! They miss the most crucial point for those with an FASD: when memory is compromised, justice delayed is justice denied. Not only that, many support people and witnesses are giving up time and energy they might need for other obligations. Work, for instance. Family, for instance.

Tim stomped in at supper time having had, as he said, "A day of turmoil!"

He had lost two packs of cigarettes but didn't ask me for replacement money. He used my tools to fix his bike, used the end of last night's chicken for his supper, found his favourite shirt sopping wet inside my washing machine, threatened suicide, and vanished without saying goodbye.

He called later, still grumpy. Lynn, who has a driver's license and a six-month driving ban, had stolen her mother's car and crashed it, "right after she stopped for coffee at your place, Mom."

The mother had connected with Tim to get more details of Lynn's social stop with me. I wonder what I am supposed to have done? She is charging Lynn with theft, and Lynn is hiding from the police.

Tim said, "Lynn doesn't ever behave herself unless she is with me." Big deal—she dumps him the minute heroin beckons.

Wednesday, April 20, 2016
Tim and his Legal Aid lawyer fired each other.

This man has *not* been an acceptable advocate, either as Tim's family lawyer or as his criminal lawyer, and I haven't been able to create change. Tim needed more energy and more friendliness and more support than Mr. Thompson was prepared or able to give. Mr. Thompson had trouble understanding how to deal with a client who is brain damaged. And he probably figured out, a while back, Tim had no respect for him. In any case, he said, in my presence, "I can no longer represent you."

When Tim had finished swearing and slammed out of the office, I asked Mr. Thompson what, under these circumstances, should be *my* next step. Mr. Thompson suggested counseling for Tim. Not helpful.

We've tried counseling: it has never worked. My kids with FASD don't do well—to put it mildly!—with any kind of talk therapy. Kathleen wants to do all the talking herself. Tim is too restless to listen. And Alex, with his low IQ and high self esteem, was convinced he knew it better, regardless. Over the last forty years, I've found written comments and written lists to be much more effective than a lot of talk. And a random remark, introduced into a conversation carefully and often, has the best effect of all.

Mediation will have to be cancelled, for now. Court dates will have to be put forward. Somebody (probably me) will have to find a new Legal Aid lawyer, who will take on Tim's criminal matters, and maybe a second lawyer for family matters if the first new person can't do both. And somebody (probably me) will have to go and educate the probation officer, who, we have concluded after reading his pre-sentencing report, doesn't understand *anything* about FASD.

Tim said, "You'll be wasting your energy; he won't change."

"Maybe not for you," I said. "But let's try to help the next person who has your difficulties and needs a pre-sentencing report."

Positive news at last!!! A criminal lawyer from Victoria, who has up island clients, will take Tim onto his list if the Legal Aid officials here approve him. He is forty-seven. I asked. And one of his family members has an FASD.

Friday, April 22, 2016

Tim forgot about organizing Legal Aid. I went, but we couldn't accomplish much without him. It was the nice First Nations secretary again; the one who was so kind to both of us last year. She said they'll be happy to authorize the new Victoria lawyer as soon as Tim remembers to get in there and sign the papers.

There is a new form to be filled in: "Why do you want a different lawyer?" I would love Tim to write, "Because this one wouldn't do his work, and he got ticked off when the judge made him look bad, and it wasn't hard." But the safe and true answer is, "My lawyer said he didn't want to represent me."

And more bad news: Tim fell off his bike (again) and he thinks he has broken his other collarbone.

He announced, "And I'm NOT going to the doctor."

Later he said, "I would feel stupid, going back, when I'm not supposed to be riding my bike."

The clavicle brace he was required to wear constantly has gone missing. However, he has an appointment on Monday to have last week's collarbone break checked, and I'll try to get a word to his doctor about the new break. If it *is* a break. Tim says it is, and he has had more experience of busted bones, especially clavicles, than most of us.

Monday, April 25, 2016

Tim and I were organized to see his doctor, but first we had to make a stop to collect his backpack. He had left it with a friend. He keeps clothing and other belongings in at least ten different places around town.

I waited in the car while Tim went into the scruffiest, most broken down doorway of a garbage strewn, low-cost housing complex. Behind him, a police car pulled up and unloaded a passenger, who crept in through the same doorway. She was followed by the officer; neither reappeared.

Eventually Tim came out, carrying his backpack, but we couldn't go on to the doctor because "Lynn is hiding in there. I have to make sure she is OK."

Then Lynn gave us a frantic signal from an upstairs balcony.

But the officer was settled downstairs. He wasn't searching for Lynn—he was waiting for his passenger to collect her movable possessions and had started helping her shift boxes outside.

I said, "If your friend with the yellow stripes wanted Lynn, he would have found her by this time, and locked her in his car while he waited for the other lady."

Tim has a little bit more reasoning ability than many folks with an FASD and was reluctantly willing to move on to the doctor's office.

I had a chance for a quiet word with the receptionist regarding the possible second shoulder injury and as a result was invited in for the whole appointment. My son, when asked, said yes, he wanted his mother to come with him. This is a tad unusual, in a big man of forty. The doctor required a complete history and has agreed to be Tim's primary care physician.

Tim has indeed snapped his other collarbone: for the second time he has had two breaks in one week. This is his twelfth busted bone. No doubt his present diet and lifestyle are contributing to his deficient bone density. But what about that greenstick fracture of his leg when he was three, the fragmented arm at eight, the toe, the ankle, the ribs, and all the broken collarbones which everyone, including his doctor, put down to bad karma and general clumsiness. They said, "Accident-prone." Wish I could go back and insist on bone density testing if it was even available in those early years.

The doctor told him to go straight up to x-ray. Not a chance. Tim wanted to get back to Lynn, and he would have hopped out of my car and broken something else if I'd headed north when he wanted to go south. He says he will go for the x-ray "sometime."

I went back to the probation officer, who couldn't talk about his client due to the Privacy Act but who was very willing to listen while I talked. *If* we ever finish with court, and *if* this PO keeps Tim on his caseload, then we will work together on secure housing for him.

Also went to what used to be the welfare office—now called the Ministry of Social Development and Social Innovation which I will never remember—and did a fast presentation. I reminded them of the red flag on Tim's chart, considered necessary for life, regarding his rent direct and I shared the physical dangers he was experiencing because of trouble with landlords and unstable housing.

I was there to present an important complaint, and to work towards change, but they didn't seem to be the least bit interested.

However, because Tim had already filed my address as his place of residence, they want to send his rent for the next few months directly to me. I can't believe money could happen this easily. There has to be a catch.

I already did this kind of advocating more than twenty-five years ago. Fought the same battles, rang the same bells, pulled the same chains, and found very little support or encouragement in any of the official government systems we had to navigate.

FASD was almost unknown back then. One psychologist told me it was "Just a fad." I was seen as an unsatisfactory parent who was much too involved in my son's life and interfering with his independence.

Now they see me as an old lady in an extremely difficult situation and what can they do to help? Same clients: same workers: same problems. But my white hair and wrinkles and cane are making a huge difference. Too bad I didn't send my elderly mother into the fray with Tim when he was being a juvenile delinquent, instead of going myself.

Tuesday, April 26, 2016

I can't believe it! That ex-lawyer, Mr. Thompson, lied in court! Where do you go? … What are you supposed to do?… when a lawyer lies in front of a judge?

Last week, I was in the room when Mr. Thompson said, "I can no longer represent you."

Tim had said, "Good!" and had added some singularly rude remarks.

But today, in court, Mr. Thompson told the judge Tim had made the decision, "and would be represented by somebody else from now on."

Then he went to the courtroom door, but he didn't go out; he wanted to hear what my son had to say.

I wish Tim had called him a liar!

I wish I had bravely stood forth and protested. But court is intimidating and Tim has often said, "Mom, don't say one word. It'll be contempt of court, and they won't let you come back, and I need you."

Today's list had Tim at 10:30 a.m., but he was summoned at 9:35 and, even with Mr. Thompson's interference, we were finished and out of the courtroom in five minutes. We have to come back in May with the new lawyer.

I thought Tim would need duty counsel this morning, as this is the first day the new lawyer has been authorized through Legal Aid, and he hasn't received any paperwork yet. But the new lawyer had already phoned the Crown Counsel's office, established himself, and shifted Tim to next month.

Crown raised another matter: "Possible breach of probation and the police are investigating."

Thank goodness Tim had told me about his "possible breach" of the no contact order and I had immediately written to the police chief, the probation officer, Crown Counsel, the mediator, and several lawyers. It was another incident of the ex-girlfriend first beckoning him over, with smiles, for a little chat with his sons, and later reporting him for communicating and interacting with her instead of walking on.

I doubt if the police are "still investigating" but, on the other hand, they could arrive at any moment with a warrant for breach. You never can tell which way the law will leap.

The ex-girlfriend and her sister were at the courthouse. When we left, they were outside in a car, waiting for Tim to be summoned at 10:30 a.m. They didn't see us. They have a lot to discover about how the legal system operates.

Sunday, May 1, 2016

Tim was standing by my front door, wrapped in a big sopping towel when Woocher and I got home from our early morning walk. He was wet to the skin and freezing cold; he'd been out all night, lost in the woods by the river. He said the group he was camping with had moved their tents two hundred yards downriver, and he had searched for them in the dark until he was thoroughly lost.

Then it was suddenly daylight and the police officers were there, asking questions and calling an ambulance. He had refused the ambulance; one of the officers drove him to my house.

When the officer had asked where his mother lived and had looked on her digital map, she said, "Are you sure?" At the turn off into my strata, and once more at the house, she checked. Tim could tell she had expected to have to drive way out to the reserve and was doubtful about leaving him at the wrong place.

I phoned the cop shop and asked if the officer who delivered Tim to my door could call me. She did, and she was obliging and easy to get on with; he must have kept his cool for a change.

Not sure about the sequence of events here. The officer said Tim was sober and had a first-rate pair of lungs. She told me he yelled for help; they heard him crashing through brush and he yelled louder. She was the one who phoned for an ambulance.

Tim said he remembered falling on his bad shoulder. (His bad shoulder is the second broken collarbone from when he fell off his bike; the one not yet x-rayed.) But most of his night was a blank. He woke up under a log, cold and wet, with no memory of getting there. Heroin, in all likelihood, but could any of this be connected to his concussion last February? I remember Alex had a terrible time with post concussion syndrome the year he was fourteen.

The paramedics had given Tim two flat bags—the kind you are supposed to fold to make them heat up. They were comforting while he waited for me to get home. He ate breakfast and then went to bed where he groaned in his sleep, worrying Woocher no end.

He went back to the river, later on, and searched for his bike, his cigarettes, his wallet, and his ID, in that order. He didn't find any of them.

The bike and the cigarettes aren't my priorities, but lost ID always involves me. And my debit card. Too bad new ID and new status cards can't be ordered by the truckload. We just finished regrouping Tim's ID following the head hammering exploit.

Wednesday, May 4, 2016

Alleluia!! (I think.) Tim has moved out.

He got up at 5 a.m. and phoned a friend with a room. The friend said, "Yes you can come here." Tim proceeded to regroup his assorted boxes, then he did his planning.

His plan: fill Mom's crawl space with everything he owns except his clothes, have Mom get the rent money out of her bank account, have Mom drive both money and clothes to the new room before 11 a.m., have Mom make a second trip with bike and backpack.

He forgot to include my schedule in his planning.

That deposit for rent was supposed to come to me, to cover Tim's expenses, but I never expected to be able to use it for his expenses. Since he is living with a family member, no more than $375 per month is approved for rent. He had already promised that much to Frankie, the new 'landlord,' for May's rent. But the money was not yet in my account and I wasn't about to give any cash to Tim.

I said I was willing to give Frankie a postdated cheque and make him sign for it. Then when the rent money came into my account for this month, Frankie could cash his cheque and the money would go to him instead of to me. Tim had to either agree with this or change his plans. I knew Frankie wouldn't care how he got his money.

Tim's $375 rent will keep on coming to me, hopefully, and I will be able to continue handing it on to Frankie or whoever. Tim is appreciative; it gives him more to spend than if he was paying the $600 rental fee most people in his circumstances have to pay. And I like it because the money will go to the landlord, direct, meaning Tim has a roof. Best of all—he couldn't pester me into handing him cash.

Thursday, May 5, 2016

Since Tim's main problem, apart from using illegal drugs, is housing (in my opinion; not his) one of this day's calls went to the homeless shelter. I asked for the executive director, a lady, brisk and efficient. She said Tim would have to go to the shelter in person, talk to her, and fill in all their forms. They offer support for the paperwork. They could then help him with barriers such as housing and getting onto a disability pension.

I said, "Housing is my reason for calling. Tim already gets a disability pension. He has brain damage: FASD."

There was a less confident pause, and then she said, "Have you spoken to the FASD Association here in town?"

I said, "I am the FASD Association here in town! ... and I need help!"

Another FASD parent told me about a similar incident she experienced at a planning meeting when her daughter was a teenager. The authorities had no services to offer, and they were not particularly kind to the mother, either.

Then they said, "You might want to talk to this woman. She's very knowledgeable about FASD, and we hear she's easy to work with," and they handed across a card – with her own phone number on it.

When the possibility of housing through the homeless shelter was mentioned to Tim, he said, "I can't go *there*! I need to get *away* from drugs!"

Sunday, May 8, 2016

Tim spent part of the night in Emergency. He had overdosed and had woken up to police officers and paramedics. Thank God he had used with friends; they realized what was happening and dialed 911. Someone had injected Narcan into him before the ambulance got there. Most street people carry a naloxone kit and most of them have needed to use the contents on their friends. They get the kits free through Harm Reduction.

The dispatcher told Tim's friends how to do artificial resuscitation, putting pressure on the chest. Tommy did it, and he said he could feel ribs crackling under his hands.

Another frantic call to the first responders, who said, "Do it anyway!!" and "We're nearly there."

They told Tim he had been more or less dead for twenty minutes. Face grey, lips blue, barely breathing.

He says he had a terrible scare—so did I!—and he plans to go back to beer and marijuana. To add to his snapped collarbones, he now has cracked ribs from the resuscitation. I'm told this is a common complaint among folks who overdose and survive.

I am thankful for free naloxone kits, but I believe it's time for my government to follow the money and clip off the extra tip of this illegal drug pyramid.

Tim and his friends, who have reached the stage of overdosing on the streets, are either dealing drugs themselves in a small way, or, more likely, they are stealing to support their habits. Tim told me he has to sell his stolen stuff to a "fence" (a receiver of stolen goods) for less than half of what it is really worth, to get enough money for drugs.

Then the fence sells online to ordinary people who are hunting for bargains. Tim says drugs on the street can lead to remarkable deals for the rest of us.

His comment: "For us addicts, there's no point in stealing if you can't sell to a fence. You sure can't push a 'borrowed' lawnmower through town to the feet of organized crime and demand your twenty bucks."

Looking at the whole illicit drug scene, I have decided the fences are at the center of the problem. If there were no markets for stolen goods, then the fences would go broke and maybe leave town. And if there were no fences buying stolen property, the stealing would stop. And if there was no money here for drugs, then the big drug lords would have to find a new market somewhere else.

Might not make much difference for Tim and his friends, at this stage, but getting rid of the fences could help prevent the younger kids from starting on drugs. That's what my son thinks, and I agree with him.

Tuesday, May 10, 2016

Zan told Tim he is going to make a fascinating skeleton at the end of his life. An important college of physicians and surgeons will be getting all the breaks.

Monday, May 23, 2016

Kathleen and Pooh met Woocher and me at the off leash park yesterday afternoon for a walk beside the river. Afterwards, Kathleen said she would like to come by for coffee. She wanted to help with early pricing and prepping for the church bazaar, which is planned for September. Help is precious! I would never say, "No thanks."

But Woocher and Pooh, who generally behave when they are inside together, pestered each other continually. They both wanted the biggest dog bed. There are *four* dog beds in my house.

Kathleen stayed for an early supper. We did another short dog walk, with Pooh being noticeably uncooperative.

And it wasn't over yet. Kathleen called at 6 p.m., to tell me Pooh had been sick "all over the carpet." She left a message at 7:15 asking what she should feed Pooh; he seemed to be hungry. When I got home from Mahjong at 8:30, she was frantic—should she take Pooh to the local vet or the one in Nanaimo?

Then Tim arrived at 9:15 p.m., unusually fed up with himself. He and his friend, Dallas, had been cooking spaghetti and had accidentally spilled it into the campfire.

I organized a thermos of hot soup for two, buns with cheese, fruit, cookies, and pop, and sent him on his way, rejoicing.

Today was quiet. Kathleen got in touch once to give me Pooh's health report, and Tim left ten minutes ago with supper for three and a plan to move camp.

The new criminal lawyer, Stefano Esposito, has arranged to have a telephone chat with Tim, here, tomorrow at 11:15 a.m. Sure hope that works out with no complications.

Wednesday, May 25, 2016

Kathleen and I experienced harassment—or maybe it was intimidation—in the school woods.

Pooh and Woocher, happily following rabbits, had gone through the woods and out the other side onto private property where we couldn't see them. There is no fence; the dogs had no way of knowing they were trespassing. The landowner of the next property saw the dogs and chased after their owners. When he caught up, he stood almost on top of me. He was vibrating with anger, and a vein on his forehead was bulging. Pooh and Kathleen and I were yelled at and threatened, but Woocher had been grabbed. The man said he had locked "your damn dog" in a shed and was planning to drown him in the river. I started to shake, Kathleen started to cry, and we both had to restrain Pooh who was anxious to head up a protest with teeth in it.

Just before we got ourselves out of the woods and back onto the main road, Woocher joined us. He wasn't wet; he had been released from the shed.

We plan to walk at the dike from now on. We don't want to be responsible for the stroke that man will have if he sees us again.

I'll have to make the school aware, as we have been the after-hours guardians of their woods for the last few years and have reported fires, overnighters, neighbourhood children building bicycle jumps, and pellet gun parties. We also pick up garbage, keep the trails clear of windblown branches, and make a point of being friendly with the teenage pot smokers who hang out at the top of the trail.

Friday, May 27, 2016

A year after being harassed and threatened, the ex-girlfriend finally had her day in court. Tim will not be going to jail. He will have eighteen months of probation with conditions: keep the peace, be of good behaviour, no drugs or alcohol, distance himself from his ex, stay out of pubs and liquor stores.

We were in court for an hour, and the ex's victim impact statement used up more than thirty minutes of the time. Not sure why we needed this, since Tim had already pleaded guilty for breaking some of his own furniture and threatening domestic assault.

The ex-girlfriend delivered a list, straight out of the dictionary *and* in alphabetical order, of words describing how she had felt when she was threatened and terrorized. The judge protested at the letter "P" with, "Thank you. I understand."

She had to take little breaks for a sob and a drink. She got large parts of her personal history wrong; I was aware of her mistakes because this is Tim's history, too.

She went back to her chair, drooping and dramatic, but she looked terrific, very tall and professional in a dark green suit and high heels.

Moments later, when restitution was mentioned, she bounced back up to the front, smiling and full of bright ideas.

We had to wait at the courthouse for the probation orders to come through and be signed. Tim was supposed to take them to the probation office but he said he would do it tomorrow. Now he was going to get drunk.

I said, "Are you sure this is a sensible plan?"

Tim said, "I know what I'm doing, Mom."

Haven't seen him since.

Tuesday, May 31, 2016

A family lawyer at last—Skye Smith. She works out of the same Victoria office as the new criminal lawyer.

Legal Aid gave Tim this name three weeks ago. He made a trip to the courthouse to sign everything, and we were told the forms had already been sent to Ms. Smith.

But when we were in court, last Friday, Stefano told Tim he had to do the "family lawyer" paperwork, and then Legal Aid could give Skye Smith the official go-ahead.

Obviously there has been a gap somewhere in the system. What's new?

Meanwhile, Tim has had a letter from Legal Aid in Nanaimo confirming the change of family lawyer.

Wednesday, June 1, 2016

Lynn is out, and it's nowhere near three months. I wonder who posted bail?

She and Tim came in for supper last night but they only wanted a bowl of cold cereal. Lynn texted her mother and grandma to tell them she's back in town, and she made two long distance calls (on *my* phone) and she left messages at the rehabilitation center and on her probation officer's answering machine. But mostly she and Tim were concentrating on wheeling and dealing.

A big weird electrical device, left on my patio for two months, is swiftly being organized for sale. I suspect I've been harbouring stolen goods.

They couldn't stay. Lynn has managed to get a bed at the homeless shelter and you have to be in before curfew or you lose your space. At least she is talking about rehab.

Sister Marianna dropped in and caught Tim at home. Whatever they talked about she definitely made an impression. Having a new criminal lawyer, who cares, has already made him feel way more hopeful and he said the talk with Sister Marianna was the icing on the cake. She was the social worker who apprehended Tim when he was eighteen months old, and brought him to our house. She has kept in touch with him ever since.

Lynn keeps me up to date regarding Tim's ex-girlfriend and the little boys through "street news." Mostly, I don't pay much attention because it's a rumour, and there is a lovely bumper sticker: "I survived a rumour."

But the word on the street is the twins desperately want their daddy,—which is nothing new—with a footnote: the ex is jealous of Tim.

According to Lynn, when Tim and his ex collected their sons from daycare, the boys used to run to Daddy while their mother stood there, arms out, being ignored. I already knew this, having seen it in action, but how did the street find out?

Next week Tim will be meeting his new family lawyer.

The mediator will not be available through July and August; they are trying to set up a mediation date before the end of June. Hopefully, this new lawyer will be able to organize for the little boys to see their father. Hopefully, the monthly reports the ex is supposed to provide for Tim will start being written at last.

Thursday, June 9, 2016
Outsiders are quick to tell me I am "enabling" my son. They have difficulty seeing the difference between the kinds of enabling a husband might choose to do for a wife with intelligence and alcohol addiction and the holistic support a parent has to put in place for an intelligent but brain damaged son. I would be supporting Tim, when asked, with or without his addiction issues.

If he had done this to himself I wouldn't be so involved. But he was born with brain damage, through no fault of his own, and he can't help the way his life has gone.

He has such a hard time understanding consequences, controlling impulses, processing information... and even more difficulty with time and money management...

Besides, I have learned how to set boundaries. Mostly.

Another thing outsiders are quick to tell me: "Don't use the term "brain damaged." What else am I supposed to say? This has been a problem for FASD advocates for YEARS!

My kids are not intellectually disabled, nor are they dealing with mental health issues and they don't fit under "non-traumatic acquired brain injury" because their impairment isn't considered an injury. If it was acquired before birth it doesn't count. They aren't on the list of "Brain Damages at Birth" because they got their harm before birth.

And I often feel a twinge of jealousy because my kids have never been able to get the services they need as compared with the autistic and intellectually disabled children who have huge government support.

Saturday, June 11, 2016

Came home from town to find Lynn and her friend Sharon knocking on my door.

Lynn had splintered a mirror and had four tiny cuts on her hand. "And I gashed my boob!" she announced, showing me.

As well, there was a woman on a bike shadowing them with intent to bully and they were afraid to walk back to town. And had I seen Tim? …or had he said where he was going?

My first necessity was to keep them out of the house since Tim wasn't there to watch for theft, and my second was to remove them from the strata before the conventional elderly folk I live with started to become unglued.

I asked, "What do you guys need?"

Sharon said, pathetically, "A drink."

Perfect! I said, "Hop into the car. There's a case of pop in there, and I'll take you where ever you need to go."

They drank their pop while we drove to the homeless shelter for Lynn's tent and sleeping bag. Lynn ran indoors, with promises to hurry. She didn't. Sharon wasn't entitled to go with her.

"She's too young," Lynn informed me. Kids under nineteen aren't allowed inside. You have to be of age to use the facilities or to get a bed for the night.

I said to Sharon, "Lynn has done all the talking, so far. What do *you* need?"

Sharon thought Lynn had planned to ask me for food. I remembered the ice cream bars I had bought for Tim, now quietly melting behind us. They each ate two of those, washed down with more pop, and were delivered to the river.

They said, "If you see Tim, tell him we'll be camping down at the other end."

I did see Tim. He came in for supper with a lad named Jacob, and with an interesting story concerning the adventures and disasters of Lynn. She had robbed several riverside tents, although not Tim's, for once. No wonder "a bully" was chasing her on a bike!

Wednesday, June 13, 2016

Kathleen phoned from town to tell me she had "been attacked!!" In fact, she had been yelled at by a driver indulging in road rage.

"And he tried to get into my car!" She had quickly locked the doors when she saw him coming towards her.

She was an emotional wreck but had managed to get the fellow's license number. I made her hang up on me and phone the RCMP instead.

The officers came at once and were very understanding and supportive. They told her to walk around town until she stopped shaking and not try to drive her car for at least thirty minutes. They had been texted by a witness and already knew the license number of the raging man. Kathleen was pleased and grateful a stranger had helped her.

Tuesday, June 21, 2016

Tim and I met his new family lawyer, Skye, at the Duncan courthouse. There was nowhere to talk inside and it was cold and windy outside.

Skye said, "Let's go down to Timmy's and get a coffee." An excellent choice—busy and noisy; nobody could overhear our conversation.

We talked for ages. Skye asked multiple questions and paid attention to our answers. She had the court files, and I gave her another stack of papers, but she hadn't done any reading because she wanted to meet Tim first.

She said she would talk to the ex-girlfriend's lawyer and try to find out why the visits aren't happening. She and Tim both hope to get matters moving without going to court. But Tim thinks his ex is dead keen to get back in front of a judge. He says the more she can share concerning his evilness, the happier she will be.

Tim has a new probation officer; he met her today. He didn't need me, and I haven't heard much about their meet and greet except he has to see her again in two weeks. There is never enough opportunity to build a relationship with any of these professionals. You barely get used to one and he's gone.

And I paid the government too much income tax. A cheque from Revenue Canada was in my mailbox, returning half of what I sent them. Yes!

Wednesday, June 22, 2016

Tim and Lynn dropped in this evening and stayed until 10:15 p.m. They came very late, still hoping for supper, and Lynn was suffering from a toothache.

She wanted Rice Krispies, but the last box was emptied yesterday; she had to eat Corn Flakes.

She wanted a chicken burger. I said, "Sorry, this isn't a restaurant. I can offer bread and cheese."

She wanted butterscotch ice cream but that was also finished. She got strawberry ripple instead and happily mixed it with chocolate hail.

She wanted my tweezers to fix her eyebrows.

"No."

But I did give her Tylenol for her toothache.

Sunday, June 26, 2016

There is a national FASD conference next week and I'm supposed to be one of the speakers. Right after that, Calgary, and a visit with Cricket and Clay and grandchildren. Then a camping trip here on the island with Zan and Bedelia and more grandchildren. Two holidays in a row! This week I am trying to do all the preparation for myself, Tim, and Woocher.

Skye wrote, "We need to get these visits started. Do you think Tim could get himself organized without your help if it was at the park downtown?"

I wrote back, "He would have good intentions. But knowing the damage he has in the areas of planning and carrying through, I'm afraid a first visit without any support would set him up for failure."

Saturday, July 2, 2016

Another heroin overdose! I can't believe it. Tim said he was going back to beer and marijuana. Guess he needed something stronger.

If only there was a way for him to get a prescription from his doctor for exactly the right amount of clean, safe heroin. Other sick people get prescriptions for what they need—why not people with addictions?

Tim needs some kind of system in place that would let him report to a nursing station once or twice daily for a free shot. I keep thinking of the savings on *my* taxes, now being spent for harm reduction, overdose prevention, ambulances, first responders, visits to Emergency, arrests, courts, jails… The other day I heard a statistic on the radio: every street person with addictions using all those services on a regular basis costs the taxpayers $20,000 per year. I'll bet free heroin wouldn't cost that much, per citizen with addictions, per year.

If Tim knew that clean heroin was available for him, as needed, he wouldn't have to steal anything. He wouldn't be arrested for theft or possession. He wouldn't need ambulance and Emergency services. If his heroin was considered a medicine and provided free of charge, even my income tax would notice the difference.

The police force could go back to sorting out real criminals instead of spending so much time on petty theft. The receivers of stolen goods, and the big dealers, and the heroin providers working through organized crime would go out of business. That would suit me!

If Tim didn't have to concentrate on getting high every day he could probably get back to work. He has always enjoyed heavy labour. Instead of wasting taxes, he could be *paying* taxes.

With clean heroin available to him daily he could lead a normal life. Why can't my government get hold of that? As my kids would say, "It isn't rocket science!"

Monday, July 25, 2016

Tim stayed here for three days, mostly asleep. Don't see how he can sleep so extensively. I suspect he was out on the loose partying during the nights but leaving my door unlocked to be sure he could get in easily at dawn. I'm glad Woocher is here.

Yesterday, he went back to his camp. Too bad he didn't stay for one more day. He was supposed to be meeting Skye at the courthouse this morning at 10 a.m. She has to be sure he understands and agrees with what she is advising before she files his documents.

Skye called me at 10:30 a.m. No Tim. She has to be back at the courthouse tomorrow and could meet him at 10:30 if I can get a message to him. I am so grateful for her grasp of Tim's special needs.

He came in with Lynn at noon, in pursuit of lunch. They were both sorry about missing the meeting. They had slept in. Tim had counted on Lynn to wake him up, and she didn't.

I said, "I'm not the person you need to apologize to." Lynn's face remained blank, but Tim asked if he could use my computer.

He sent an apologetic email to Skye, told her 10:30 tomorrow morning "would be excellent," and added, "I will stay at Mom's place tonight to be organized and ready."

Tim is going through a bad patch, which gives me a little bit of room to be supportive. When life is going well for him he is much less interested in paying attention to my views.

Thursday, July 28, 2016

Grief counseling yesterday, and Tim seemed peaceful afterwards. He sees the new criminal lawyer today. He is here with me, sharing a cup of coffee but not breakfast. He ate bacon and eggs at the Breakfast Club following his first night back in his tent.

We have survived what I understand is termed cold turkey. Not fun, and uncommonly messy.

Tim is presently regrouping his belongings, smiling, and speaking clearly instead of mumbling. Hope of seeing his sons at last has helped considerably. A new visit supervisor has been chosen by the ex-girlfriend and will be paid by a member of Tim's Team.

Monday, August 1, 2016

One of my friends, parenting an FASD grandson, told me, "My grandson was walking home in the dark, hitchhiking. He texted me that he had a stomach ache. No one was picking him up and he was thinking of jumping into the traffic, the pain was so bad.

"I was going to go and get him and drive him home but his aunt offered to go, instead. He yelled at her the whole way. When he got here he punched the door, breaking three bones in his hand—and that's his normal behaviour."

I was reminded of our Tim. He has also cracked and dislocated his hand bones twice, punching walls.

After the first smash …it was about seventeen years ago… he saw an outstanding plastic surgeon and his right hand mended beautifully. With the second round, in summer, his bones didn't align properly because he cut off the cast to go swimming. He gets a stab of pain up to the elbow when he tries to lift anything heavy with his left hand.

It could have been worse; he could have punched somebody's head.

Wednesday, August 10, 2016

Kathleen and Pooh stayed with me for a long weekend because they had another rat. It got in through a crack in her bathroom wall. She spray filled the new hole, herself, and asked Uncle Bruce to reset the traps.

They have gone back home and Pooh is relaxed; therefore his owner can relax. Kathleen's building has cockroaches at the far end, bats living inside at her end and rats throughout. There are rumours her building manager is going to be fired.

Thursday, August 25, 2016

Tim had two short prison terms this summer, both of them when I wasn't at home.

He was breached for missing appointments with his probation officer. He had his day in court this week, and told duty counsel, "I *had* to breach my probation! What else did they expect me to do?"

Duty Counsel reminded the court that Tim wasn't able to see his probation officer or contact his drug and alcohol counselor or even be present in this courtroom, legally, because his previous order said he couldn't be "east of the highway." A perfect excuse! During his last court appearance, the judge, Crown, and lawyer were all from out of town and unfamiliar with our city layout.

Today they sent one of the court secretaries for a map of the whole municipality. It was spread out on the front table; judge, Crown, sheriff, duty counsel, and secretary crowded around. The mistake has been corrected. Tim can go anywhere he needs to be—he was doing that, anyway—with nothing but the home of his ex-girlfriend off limits.

The confusing part for me: as far as I could tell, Tim didn't plead either guilty or not guilty.

Following court, he had to sign papers at the registry office and then meet with his probation officer. The papers always take ages to get ready. We made the mistake of going for a hamburger while we waited.

At McDonald's, we met a look-alike of Tim's ex-girlfriend. She was tall, thin, blond, pierced, tattooed, and high; she told us, "Lynn is in big trouble."

Lynn has to steal for drug money and this time she chose the wrong target. Once Tim had heard that, I barely managed to get him back to the court registry to sign his order. He had no interest in seeing the probation officer. He had to save Lynn. More drama—they can't live without it.

I try to accept Tim as he presents himself, regardless, because so many people are unsympathetic and unsupportive but I did ask, "Do you really want to see your kids?"

"Yes, of course!"

"Then make sure you get yourself to the PO's office. Today!"

His second trip to jail, during my second holiday, occurred because he got into trouble with the police for shoplifting following a playtime with his little boys. Likely this wouldn't have happened if he could have come to me and let off steam. There's another court date coming up for Theft Under.

Then he used crystal meth to keep himself off more heroin and overdosed again. Thankfully he was with two adult, non-addicted friends. They revived him safely, and both told me, later and separately, he could easily have died without their care.

It's taken a while to change direction but family and friends are finally coming to terms with how serious this is. For the first time, I'm wondering if Tim is going to survive …

Saturday, August 27, 2016

While the summer weather lasts, playdates for Tim and his sons are being held outside, on the grounds of one of the local churches. This is a pleasant place to meet, with swings and a slide and lots of room to run. The single drawback is the wasps. They are worse there than anywhere else I have been this summer and I'm frequently out in the bush with my dog.

At the end of yesterday's playtime while Tim and the little boys were saying goodbye, I had a chat with Supervisor A. When I said how much the kids and Tim love each other, Supervisor A said, "Yes, that's obvious."

Tim has been given a copy of his ex-girlfriend's Rules for Visits. Supervisor A told him he is expected to sign and return same. He will attend to it with Skye when she is back. Hopefully, the ex will also be expected to sign in front of her lawyer as most of these rules apply to both parents.

Tuesday, September 6, 2016

And a letter for me from the Ministry of Justice. I looked at the return address and thought, "Now what has he gone and done?" But it wasn't about Tim; it was about me, and it was very annoying.

"We have recently received an unsolicited report concerning your fitness to drive. We require further information regarding your medical status. You will soon receive in the mail a Driver's Medical Examination Report. You have 45 days…"

I phoned the number on the letter—it said Ministry of Justice but it was actually for Road Safety BC—and told a pleasant voice I had no idea what my problem could be, but since I wear glasses should I see my eye doctor first?

He said, "No. Your family doctor will do a referral if necessary."

I asked, "And can I expect to be repeating this medical examination frequently? …because the person who made the unsolicited report to you is not the biggest leaf on the tree."

He laughed, and said, "No. We will not accept another report from the same person."

When I called my own doctor's office to make an appointment, her receptionist said, "Is the line on the form blue or green or yellow?"

I said, "Blue."

She said, "Excellent! Blue means the government pays." In other words, the taxpayers.

And when I handed my doctor the Driver's Medical Examination Report to be filled in, she said, "Who is your enemy?"

Tuesday, September 20, 2016

A nice change this week: for the first time Tim got to have his whole two hours with his sons. The ex-girlfriend's hand is firmly in place and her controls dominate but not quite as heavily as two months ago when nobody was allowed to sneeze without her permission.

Wednesday, October 5, 2016

The weather is getting mighty cold and the river is rising. Soon all the illegal tent sites will be underwater.

We have been searching for an apartment for Tim. He said he wants to have his own address. This is a step in the right direction.

Woocher is supposed to be having two baths a week, using expensive shampoo from the vet to control his allergic reactions. It's getting too cold to bathe him outside and besides, my garden hose will soon have to be stored for the winter and the outside taps will be turned off. There is no way I can get him into my tub—ninety pounds of flat refusal. We drove downtown to The Doggy Bath. The workers there are pleasant, the baths are at the right level for the humans doing the work and Woocher didn't complain.

They have a blow-dry system. We left a pound of hair at Doggy Bath and have since spread another pound around the house. Add dog hair to the river sand Tim and his friends bring in on their feet and I could plant potatoes under my kitchen table.

Monday, October 10, 2016

A call from the criminal lawyer. He was phoning with regard to Tim's next court appearance later this week.

Tim has two items pending.

His breach of the order preventing his going east of the highway is still waiting to be resolved. This mistake on the part of the Legal System was corrected but left unfinished. He has to deal with it and his lawyer told him to plead not guilty. The other charge was for shoplifting; I think a chocolate bar. Or that might have been a different incident.

These matters were both on the court list a few weeks ago. Tim and I were there, and the ex-girlfriend was also there, but Stefano didn't come. He had put the case forward three weeks but had forgotten to tell Tim. The sheriff told us; we left.

But the ex stayed until the bitter end. Then she went to the court registry office and demanded to be given the reason why Tim hadn't been called upon, "since his name is on the list."

The court secretary couldn't tell her much, so she marched off to the Crown Counsel's office, wanting to be told why she "hadn't been informed since she had given up a day's work," and angrily insisting on immediate answers to all her questions.

And why would anybody tell her anything? … she is completely uninvolved.

Tim's lawyer has been in touch with Crown Counsel who are, in reality, the opposition, but this particular Crown is lovely. They have sensibly decided to delete Tim's breach charges and go with the shoplifting. And they want him to plead guilty and get a minimum fine with no probation.

The lawyer told me their general opinion: the probation system isn't doing much for Tim. One of our friends, who is part of Tim's Team, sits beside him during every appointment. With so much backing and with a caring family living in the same town, the authorities feel Tim doesn't need to be supported by probation. His PO has already extended his appointments to once every three weeks, although once a week is usual.

That's not all. They have put Tim's court forward. The date will be written into the system and will be available online, but Tim will be summoned several days beforehand and his case will be dealt with privately. This is because they are very tired of the ex-girlfriend pestering both court officials and Crown counsel staff members with questions about subjects that are none of her business.

The Crown said, "She is distressing Tim and as a result he is too tense to deal with his issues calmly."

I am thankful they have gotten hold of the baffling ways of the ex-girlfriend without any of Tim's support team having to comment officially. Couldn't believe my ears when the lawyer said, "This is how we are going to deal with Tim's ex."

Wednesday, October 19, 2016

Supervisor A sent an email saying the visit on Friday would have to be cancelled. One of the boys has been diagnosed with ringworm.

I figured cancellations for ambiguous health reasons would start happening pretty soon. The ex-girlfriend wants to be free of Supervisor A, who is suddenly "nonprofessional."

That's because Supervisor A likes Tim. She was surprised when she met him to find him such a good-natured individual and such a capable parent. She gets along nicely with me and with the rest of the team. Therefore, she has to go.

Meanwhile, the first playdate with the new private social worker, Supervisor B, went well. It was late: 5:15 until 6:45 p.m., following preschool and a karate lesson with no breaks in between. I would never have expected little kids to cope with so much but both Tim and the ex-girlfriend think I'm old-fashioned regarding rests, free time and hours of sleep for children.

Tim said Supervisor B watched and listened but stayed out of the conversations and the games between father and sons.

Hopefully this new supervisor will accept neither control nor guidance from the ex-girlfriend. And it will be super for Tim—if he gets there—to see his twins twice a week whenever their mother can't prevent the visits.

Supervisor B's time is expensive; Tim's Team will be paying her and I will take over paying Supervisor A.

Thursday, October 20, 2016

Stefano called late last night. He has to be in court this morning and the right Crown is on. Could Tim come in at 9:30 a.m. and get his matters dealt with, without certain persons knowing?

Tim definitely could.

So we went and in ten minutes there were no more charges against him. Lawyer and Crown worked together beautifully. Stefano came over and asked me how much of a fine Tim could afford; they set it at $100. That was fair since the stolen items came to about thirty-five dollars. The judge said since Tim's probation will already last till October 2017 there would be no point adding more.

When we were finished, Stefano shook my hand and said, "Well, that's it, Ruth. Call me if anything else comes up."

I said, "It will. I hope you don't plan to retire for about forty years."

Thursday, October 27, 2016

Had a disagreeable cataract repair yesterday morning. Surgery was supposed to take eleven minutes—it lasted two hours. Far more anesthetic than usual was needed. I was so sick! The same result as we used to have with ether back in the Stone Age.

Saw the eye doc today. She told me everything that could go wrong *did* go wrong during the surgery. It gave her a chance to practice every skill she had ever learned. My vision was blurry last night. Seems to be much better now.

Tuesday, November 1, 2016

I contacted Harm Reduction with a question. They give out brown paper bags of user supplies, free for all who are addicted; Tim gets his twice a week. I needed to know the best way to dispose of the alcohol wipes and ascorbic acid sachets and water vials and stericups and sharps collectors and blue plastic tourniquets and syringes (used and unused) cluttering my carport and guest room.

Because if I would die without warning, and the police officers and coroner would search the place, they would suppose I had overdosed. And I didn't.

The two ladies who run Harm Reduction came by tonight to collect my box of goodies. They gave me a naloxone kit and training on how to use it. If Tim stops breathing and gets funny looking, I'll understand how to help.

Thursday, November 10, 2016

Some sadness for Kathleen. She has been able to keep her car on the road, with difficulty, but now repairs are becoming more and more expensive. She suspects the poor old thing has almost reached its last gasp.

Wednesday, November 23, 2016

Welfare Wednesday: Tim might not manage his 5:15 p.m. visit with the twins. And I'm not sure if he got there last week, either.

As a general rule he comes here first, has a shower, changes his clothes and I drive him into town. He can't go on his bike because there is no safe place to leave it. We used to go at 5:05 but daylight saving time has been changed back to standard, and now we have darkness at 4:45. Because of not being able to drive safely at night, I have to take Tim to Supervisor B's office building much too early. Then he has an extended wait before the kids come, and no impulse control.

Still Welfare Wednesday.

Tim has handled his day remarkably well, with no incapacitating drug use. He was here at noon wanting breakfast, with Lynn in tow. Not surprising. Lynn is always very visible on Welfare Wednesdays.

In spite of my doubts regarding today's visit, Tim came back on his bike at 4:45 p.m. and collected snacks and juice for himself and the little boys. He doesn't need my rides anymore. Supervisor B, as soon as she understood our transportation problem, told him he could bring his bike inside the building.

He came again at 7:30, with Jules, to pick up various belongings. He said he'd had a fabulous playtime with his kids.

Friday, November 25, 2016

As of this morning, Tim is renting my spare room upstairs until he can go back to camping at the river. This is official; his rent is coming to me directly from the Ministry and not going into his bank account. Hope it works out—for both of us.

Tim carried his big bookshelf and all his boxes up to my guest room. I cleared and cleaned the garage and parked my car indoors for the first time since he got hit on the head with a hammer last February. He is now upstairs, doing what he terms "sorting and organizing," and what I think of as equalizing the mess.

There is still a foreign banana box shelved in my garage.

Tim said, "That's Lynn's box. I don't know anything about it."

I had a look inside. No needles, no dead food, no mouldy socks, mostly just her art supplies and some clean summer clothes. At the bottom of the box, carefully wrapped in a plastic bag, was the Christmas card I had sent her last year when she was in Alouette Detention.

Saturday, December 3, 2016

I sent this email to the kids and also to myself. There are times when it pays to be able to remember exactly what was said.

> Hi Guys
> This is about St. Nicholaas.
> Not sure when any of you are planning to arrive; shall we do lunch at 12:30 p.m.?
> The Christmas sugar cookies have been baked and are waiting to be decorated. I hope a few of the children can come early to ice them; that will give the icing lots of time to become firm. Then you can each take your share home and I won't have to sort and pack later. Yes!
> Is anybody interested in decorating the outside crab apple tree? The little silver balls have new ribbons, tied and ready to hang.

I don't intend to set up and decorate my inside tree, this year. If any of you want Mom/Ruth/Oma to have a Christmas tree, it will be up to you to organize.

A blessed St. Nicholaas Day to everybody!

Wednesday, December 7, 2016

Tim has just lost another friend. Jacob overdosed and died on the Dwyer School steps last night, during an evening event. Tim spent much of the morning in tears. And I twisted my knee while walking Woocher. Between us we were not in great condition to meet Skye at the courthouse.

We had to fill in a difficult form: Tim's budgeting of his disability pension with a view to paying child support. But Skye says as long as he has to pay for unnecessary supervision, he shouldn't be required to cover child support as well. If the twins were coming to my place twice a week to see Daddy, then he might have to cough up a small amount.

This would be a terrible choice for the ex-girlfriend. To get the money, she would have to let her kids have an uncontrolled playtime with Public Enemy #1 at the home of Public Enemy #2. Keeping the controls in her own hands (she sees it as keeping her children safe) means no extra money in her pocket.

When the work at the courthouse was done, Skye said, "We're going for lunch and I'm buying."

Another lawyer said, "Skye, you're making the rest of us look really bad!"

Tim managed to stop crying about Jacob, once he had polished off a delicious meal and three cups of strong coffee. He had a playdate scheduled with the little boys at 5:15 p.m. and left my place at 4:45, with his backpack full of St. Nicholaas treats. I sure hope he made it.

Thursday, December 8, 2016

He made it! Supervisor B sent me the Christmas schedule changes by email and she said she had given them to Tim in writing.

Apart from Jacob's unexpected death, Tim is thriving at this time. He's hanging out at the old boarding house. He and the landlord who hit him with his hammer are working together, sanding furniture for sale, and Tim is getting paid a bit. I'm seeing a lot less of him and when he is here he's pleasant.

Monday, December 12, 2016

Snow. Cold and dreary and exceedingly slippery. I've had three falls. One was nasty; I hurt my knee and it has been a little bit sore ever since. But yesterday (the fifth day following the accident) my leg was covered with dark purple bruises down to the ankle. And now I've got burning behind my knee.

The nurse at 811 said, "See a doctor. Now!" and, "You shouldn't be walking!"

Bruce said he would drive me to the clinic.

Tuesday, December 13, 2016

My knee will be fine; what's wrong with it is a Baker's Cyst. Something inside has split a little bit, and fluid is coming into places where fluid shouldn't be. That's what is causing the pain and bruising. (I'm reasonably sure this is how the doctor explained it.)

I can be active as long as the activity doesn't hurt. If it hurts I have to stop doing it. My doctor said the bruises will darken and my leg will feel worse before it starts to get better. Eventually it will improve on its own.

Tuesday, December 20, 2016

Tim was at McDonald's with friends when his ex-girlfriend came in. She is supposed to leave if she sees him, but she called him over. At first he looked the other way and didn't budge but the youngsters weren't with her and she kept on calling so eventually he went across.

The ex said, "I'm sorry about all the supervision but I have to do it because the kids come first."

Tim said, "I would do the same thing in your place."

He has never resented the supervision he is inflicted with although it would be a very different story if paying for it was coming out of *his* money.

They also talked about Tim's drug use. He told her he is almost off heroin and she must have been able to see that for herself; he has gained a lot of weight.

It sounds as if they had a positive meeting with a lot of Christmas goodwill—but the ex will use everything Tim said to her advantage.

Friday, December 23, 2016

Had to cancel my plans for a noontime Christmas dinner for at least three people. My knee and leg are not improving; last Wednesday my doctor said, "Elevate." Can't elevate and also prepare a Christmas dinner with all the trimmings. I put the turkey back into the freezer. It had hardly started defrosting after only one day in the fridge.

Kathleen will come anyway for soup and a sandwich and we'll watch a movie; then she can walk both dogs. I told Tim that he and his friends are welcome to come for lunch and indulge in a light, frothy movie (no horror) but we won't be eating turkey. We'll have the turkey dinner in January when my leg stops looking like a stovepipe.

Tim said, "I can cook the turkey," but when he remembered the rest of it— making stuffing and gravy and cranberry sauce; baking potatoes and steaming vegetables; having everything ready at the same moment—he backed off.

Monday, December 26, 2016

Went to the Christmas Eve vigil, and decided I much prefer the Christmas morning service. The change was made to accommodate my family.

Kathleen hasn't got wheels anymore; she and Pooh walked over on Christmas morning. Tim had arrived earlier, by bicycle, and had gone straight to bed. Kathleen and I enjoyed our lunch and entertained ourselves with one of her movies.

Although I was nervous about leaving Tim alone in the house, we gave our dogs a long playtime in the off leash park. Tim stayed asleep. I drove Kathleen and Pooh home before dark. Tim stayed asleep. I went and had a sumptuous dinner with an older couple from church. Tim stayed asleep.

This has been a harsh Christmas for Tim, in spite of a lovely seasonal visit with his twins on December 23. Supervisor B had her office decorated, a tree, a soft musical background of carols, and Christmas crafts for families to make together.

Afterwards, on his way back to my house, Tim stopped at McDonald's for coffee and walked in on a teenage friend who, moments before, had overdosed in the bathroom.

Word on the street: Underage youth who overdose are not treated with the same protections as adults who overdose. Tim and the individual who had administered the naloxone felt they had to get this young lad up and out of there mighty fast before either the paramedics or the officers arrived. Thanks to this rescue, Tim's crafts and cards from his little boys got left behind.

Then, continuing toward home, he came to *another* friend who was 'down' and needing to be rescued with naloxone. He told me about these adventures when he came in for breakfast on Saturday.

Early on Christmas morning Tim announced he had OD'd himself during the night.

He said, "Lynn rode my bike to a friend for naloxone and got it into me just before I died."

I thought Lynn carried a kit; she used to. Tim is trying to use less heroin but he needs extra whenever he is in an emotional uproar following playtimes with his children or following an overdose by his friends.

Because of his own OD, he slept through Christmas Day. Now he is in a *foul* mood and needing to eat constantly, as is his usual after a high.

He was distressed because of owing money for his new bike. He asked me for extra cash and was refused, issued threats, accused me of being unfair and announced he was leaving. Permanently.

He went upstairs to pack. But since then he has come back down, finished off the milk and the last of the dry cereal and is now sleeping in front of the TV.

Wednesday, December 28, 2016

Tim has been verbally abusive for the last two days.

Yesterday, I said, "Are you going to stop this or do I have to ask for outside help?"

He stomped angrily upstairs, carrying both the telephones. Bit of an empty gesture; I don't keep secrets and my neighbours are aware of our situation. Any one of them would get the police for me. And he knows that.

This morning I decided it was *my* house and I didn't have to listen anymore; I told Tim to leave. He wouldn't go. I dialed 911. The moment I started the call, he settled down and got himself packed and out.

The emergency dispatcher was superb. She stayed on the line until I had locked the door behind my son. Then two police cars pulled up; the last thing I needed, being both shaky and teary by then. But the officers were considerate. They are familiar with Tim and are aware of his FASD disabilities. One of them went and picked him up on the road and drove him into town; the other one stayed with me until I stopped shaking.

If Tim behaved this way while he was living with his ex-girlfriend and his sons, then I'm not surprised she had to ask for help to get him out of there.

Don't know if he showed up for the rescheduled visit with his boys. Normally I would have given reminders and provided the snack. There was a voice mail from Supervisor B, at what would have been about ten minutes into the visit, to tell me Tim hadn't got there yet and to ask if he was on his way.

My other kids have been wonderful—they understand Tim's problems and their support extends to me. Elaine and Kathleen both offered to come and stay for a night or two. Zan called to be sure I was safe and sound. He and Bedelia are worn out with a second baby who was supposed to be "short term." The minute our ice melts, my extra energy will go to Zan and etc. rather than to Tim and etc.

Friday, December 30, 2016

On Wednesday Tim went to see his kids at Supervisor B's office but he arrived way too early. Nobody was there. He didn't wait.

Today I saw him when we crossed paths at the pool, moments before his swim with the boys and Supervisor A.

I said, "Nice to see you," and he said, "Thanks for coming."

I'll bet he was wondering what would happen since I pay for the swimming and always bring a snack for four. He never thought ahead when he told me to stay out of his affairs.

2017

Thursday, January 5, 2017
Bedelia called to tell me one of her boys has had a seizure and is in hospital.

I've talked to Zan since then; he said the little guy is stable and they have done an ultrasound and blood tests. There was a lot of abdominal pain along with his seizure; appendicitis has been ruled out. The doctor plans to send him home tonight. He has to go to his GP next week for test results and hopefully a diagnosis. Bedelia is staying with her son, and Zan is at home with the horde.

Tim apologized once more for his behaviour last week.

I said, "Quit worrying. You told me people make remarks they don't mean when they are on drugs. And we are mostly okay. But some days I can't handle it."

Tim said, "You did the right thing."

Friday, January 13, 2017
We are rapidly going downhill, with Tim shifting back and forth between my strata and the streets. He has started coming in for meals at even weirder times than usual. His temper is iffy; I had to remind him (again) to be polite and to follow the house rules.

And for me—survival by coffee. Eating is too much effort.

Monday, January 16, 2017

Tim stayed here last night and he *didn't* sleep on the couch.
I said, "Upstairs, please," and he went without creating unrest.

But this morning he was horrid. He said, "So, what *are* the rules?" As if he didn't know!

I started with my usual, "No drugs," but there wasn't any opportunity to add, "clean up after yourself," and, "eat at the table," because it was nothing but swearing and bad temper the moment drugs were mentioned.

If I had found open, used needles, then they had fallen out of his bag. He doesn't use here; he uses in town and comes here afterwards and, "What's wrong with that?"

I told him I couldn't cope with his bad temper. He promptly decided I didn't care about him and he was adopted anyway. Nobody cared about him except his sons. In other words, his little boys are the only two people in his life who haven't complained about his drug use.

He said, "Do you want to hear how many times I died last week? I wish I was fucking dead."

I wish he could be contented, tranquil, self-controlled … but he isn't and our lives are falling apart. I need help. There is a drop-in center downtown for drug and alcohol counseling; I wonder if they will counsel a parent?

Thursday, January 19, 2017

The Drug and Alcohol receptionist started me off with a form three pages long. Name, address, and personal on the first page, health history on the second, and on the third they wanted a list of every illegal drug I have ever used. In order.

Back at the desk, I said, "The third page is blank because I'm not here for me," and she said, "I'll put a line through it," and sent me along to Chanda's office. They are used to seeing anxious parents and grandparents.

Chanda is young but she's remarkable; she has worked with FASD as well as addictions. I told her about the trouble I'm having setting rules for Tim.

She said, "We'll write a list."

My list should start with "Mom's Rules," not "Rules for Tim." And I will have to plan carefully while preparing it. Although there aren't many rules at my house, each one has to have a consequence if it isn't observed and I am responsible for the consequences.

If I write, "Mom will be available between 9 a.m. and 9 p.m," then I mustn't open the door outside of those hours, no matter how much ringing and banging and dog barking goes on.

And if I write, "Sleep on the bed upstairs, not on the couch downstairs," what happens if he refuses to go upstairs? I don't mind him using the living room couch if he is sick (e.g. concussion) or even if he is awake and resting because the TV is in there. But for sleeping off his latest dose he can use the bed and let me have the living space.

And, "Put anything you use back where you got it from," is more relevant than either, "Clean up after yourself," or "Don't take Mom's tools and kitchen equipment." My big screwdriver, both flashlights, a working potato peeler, and two ice bags have been "borrowed" without permission and a favourite bread knife vanished recently.

Chanda said, "'No drugs' includes any drugs that happen to be inside the body," and, "If he is being verbally abusive he will have to leave. You must not hesitate to dial 911."

It was a thought provoking experience. No new information, exactly, but it is helpful to have your ideas lined up and tweaked. I taped my list on the glass door where it is visible from the patio.

Mom's Rules

Mom's hours: 8 a.m. – 9 p.m.
Be polite.
Eat at the table.
Sleep on the bed upstairs. The couch is for resting and watching TV.

No alcohol or drugs at Mom's place—not in pockets or backpack or body.

Put anything you have used back where it came from.

Saturday, January 21, 2017

Tim and Ernest were here waiting for lunch when I got home. Tim had seen the list and he thought it was manageable. He was sober; what a nice difference!

Saturday, January 28, 2017

Just sent an email off to Tim's family lawyer regarding his no contact order.

He met his ex-girlfriend in town and gave her some money for the youngsters. It's nice for him to give and I'm sure the ex was happy to receive but obviously some planning happened first. From the very beginning, even before the twins were born, the ex's pattern has been to break the order herself and then to stab Tim in the back later.

When that happens, and he is charged again, we need a judge who can set up terms that will work with the way these two interact.

I asked Skye, "Is there such a person?"

Tuesday, February 7, 2017

The virus I've been blessed with this week is more than a cold. Could be a touch of flu. Feeling rotten and coughing in the night. Definitely not in any condition to keep an eye on Tim. But he is here and keeping me supplied with hot coffee. He is also taking Woocher out.

Tuesday, February 14, 2017

St. Valentine's Day

My stairs are bare and I am unconditionally impressed with my whole family! They came in a body last Sunday, and got all the old carpeting ripped off the stairs and removed from the property.

Because I'm not finished with my flu bug, they organized our lunch, set up the tables, served the food, did the dishes, walked the dog, and left the house vacuumed and tidy. I kept on sneaking back to bed.

My handyman will come soon to examine the stairs and help me decide how to recover them. Everybody else has offered an opinion; why not him? At least I'm clear about what *I* want—safety treads, contrasting colours to help with my depth perception problems, and something easy to keep clean. Too bad about resale value.

Thursday, February 16, 2017

Tim spent last night here, following a visit with his youngsters, and woke up looking for a fight. I knew any comment from me would set him off and when the misery started I asked him, "Could you please go and yell elsewhere?"

He left, and he was back in one minute, moaning and swearing. He had slipped on the ice outside the door, had landed on an upright can of Coke inside his backpack and had hurt his spine and wrist.

He is staying here and having a lot of back pain but remaining pleasant and polite. He won't entertain the idea of going to a doctor. I could insist, but it would send him off to who knows where, in this bitter weather *and* without transport as his bike has gone missing and I won't drive on ice.

Saturday, February 18, 2017

The weather is warmer and the ice is melting.

Tim left early, carrying his backpack instead of wearing it. He had a sleeping bag with him, "Just in case I don't come back."

He must be improving. The pain in his back couldn't have been as bad as it was yesterday or he would have stayed here another night.

Tuesday, February 21, 2017

Tim isn't particularly reliable or responsible, and his street friends are his priority. His lifestyle is not improving; this complicates his visitation rights. I don't think an expensive overseer is the best answer, but there has to be somebody in charge of the boys' playtimes with their father.

As a matter of fact, nobody needs to be paid. The ex-girlfriend and her parents have lots of family friends who would be willing to have the kids and Tim. Or my friends could house the group. Tim's Team would love to be involved.

We are speculating; was Supervisor A honestly sick last Friday? …or is she tired of having to cooperate with the contentious ex-girlfriend? The ex has found a justification to avoid most of the Friday visits ever since Christmas and those missing hours are never made up.

Tim is seeing his sons with Supervisor B. But if visiting times are going back to once a week, then maybe Wednesday is the option to be dropped (it is horribly expensive) and we could put our concentration into Fridays at the pool with Supervisor A.

Neither parent has legal counsel, but Skye said she would take Tim as a client immediately if the visiting schedule falls apart.

There will be another complication shortly because Tim is refusing to go back to the probation officer. I have no inkling of what went wrong there or why she isn't doing any follow-up. However, this is *not* going to become one of my problems.

I'm already busy trying to find him somewhere to live other than with me but there are still no vacancies.

Thursday, February 23, 2017

The hospital called on Tuesday night. Tim had been transported there by ambulance following a heroin overdose and would I come and pick him up? Since my night driving isn't safe, I phoned Mary Grace.

We should have let him walk. I forgot 'stable' doesn't mean 'drug free' and had assumed he was feeling ill and would go right to bed.

He didn't.

Although sick and foggy, he soon had a large plastic sheet spread out on the living room floor and was busy repairing a bicycle. I was stuck in the kitchen reading, waiting for him to go up to bed.

Suddenly he was dressed in a warm jacket and boots, organizing pink drinks and cheese buns to take along, and off to see "Buddy" who was demanding the repayment of a loan. Buddy expected him to stay for the night; they were supposed to attend at Tim's bank on Welfare Wednesday.

Apparently the loan was paid. Tim was here on Wednesday evening, relaxed and chatty. He had enjoyed an amusing playdate with his sons and shared their funny stories.

Friday, February 24, 2017

Another call from the hospital. Tim OD'd for the second night in a row and has been admitted. They are keeping him until he has seen a social worker who might be able to organize rehab.

If *he* doesn't go to rehab, I might. It would be a lovely break.

Monday, February 27, 2017

Snow started falling early. I hustled myself to Superstore before it stuck to the roads. Tim saw me driving through town, guessed where I would be, and came to pack my groceries and put them in the car. Most of the food I buy is for Tim and his friends; he was happy to see another bucket of ice cream and his favourite bulk popsicles, regardless of the weather.

He said, "When the snow is gone, can you help me get to counseling? I have to start paying attention to rehab and sober living."

I said, "Of course," but I must have looked surprised because he added, "I had a long talk with my ex."

They met "accidentally" at Starbucks. The ex-girlfriend is unfailingly able to find Tim; I'm still convinced she stalks him. But it will be wonderful if she ends up having more influence than the rest of us!

Tuesday, February 28, 2017

Tim has a new probation officer—an older man. He did not do well with his last PO, even though the team supported and attended appointments with him at his request.

I phoned this new man—his name is Basil—and found him impressive. He said he is there to build on Tim's strengths, not to recreate his weaknesses. He has no intention of being the revolving door into and out of prison. The team members can come to meetings whenever Tim wants us. And Basil will ask us to come to meetings if he anticipates extra help being needed.

Friday, March 3, 2017

Tim was supposed to see his new probation officer at 11 a.m.

He and Poppy appeared at my house at 10:55, with two loaded down bicycles, and Tim was already irritated when I opened the door. There is a clock on my windowsill facing outwards; he said he hadn't realized it was so late.

I said, "You've got your bike—unload it and you can still go," and, "I'm leaving in a few minutes." He knew I had a doctor's appointment at 11:15.

There was no breakfast on offer, and little Poppy got blessed with the resultant bad temper. When I left, moments later, there was a bike tire in the middle of the strata road. Obviously Tim had dropped it and was too mad to stop and pick it up.

Why did they ride all the way through town and out here? They could have stopped anywhere on their route and checked a clock. As far as food is concerned, they don't need to come to me for any meals except supper. The Breakfast Club is open early, and there is a nutritious lunch available at the food bank every day. Other charities provide free bread, not a gourmet meal, for sure, but nobody has to go hungry.

Tim and most of his street friends (many of whom, in my opinion, are fettered with undiagnosed FASD) have no time management skills and no forethought. And Tim is losing ground with so many overdoses.

His family isn't doing so well, either. It's the guilt. We all know there is no reason for us to feel guilty. Tim is an adult making his own decisions; what he does to himself is none of our business. We can't make him change his lifestyle. We have all done our best for him for lo these many years…

I don't know where they come from, but the little niggles of self reproach remain.

Tuesday, March 21, 2017

One of my major concerns is the way the long, lean ex-girlfriend has been stalking Tim. I felt especially uncomfortable after a chat with Lynn, who remarked casually, "She always knows where to find him."

And she does. She meets him "unexpectedly" and wants to talk. My son is such an innocent, and excessively forgiving.

He says, "She's being a lot nicer, Mom."

Of course she is … until she turns him in for breaking her latest no contact order.

Last week, at the pool, the ex-girlfriend wanted me to join her in a corner for a whispered conference. It's all about drama with the ex. I'm glad Supervisor A had already arrived and saw that I didn't instigate our conversation.

The ex had an obituary column from a Lillooet newspaper. One of the last names was the same as Tim's, pre-adoption, and she thought this person might be a dead relative.

"Do you think we should tell him?"

When did the ex-girlfriend and I return to being a "we?"

She wouldn't let me hold the paper or see the date but this person wasn't anybody I had ever heard of. And why is she getting a Lillooet paper, anyway? And why would Tim be interested? He has birth family in Lillooet but he has never been there and has firmly stated he doesn't ever want to go.

These sorts of events have been making me nervous but I couldn't figure out what to do about it because the police officers laughed when I told them, "Tim is being stalked," and because he has legal representation on such an irregular basis.

Today I had two calls from professionals. The first was from Community Living, concerned about a problem Kathleen might be grappling with. She wasn't. Then Drug and Alcohol Outreach wanted to change an appointment Tim had already made.

I put this "stalking" problem before them, as they are both in the helping professions, connecting regularly with clients who are marginalized and trivialized.

And both of them said, "Tim's probation officer needs to hear about this."

I contacted Basil and made an appointment to meet with him, feeling the whole situation was too complicated and too vague to share over the phone. But it would have been okay because Basil is First Nations. Tim hadn't mentioned that. As with my First Nations friends, he understood very quickly without needing a lot of detail.

He has got the whole dilemma written up in Tim's file. If the ex-girlfriend tries her sabotage again, he will have some protection. What a relief.

Thursday, March 23, 2017

Tim landed on me early this evening and he went straight up to bed—I hoped for the night. But now he is in the kitchen eating his third bowl of cereal and falling asleep over it. Also in it; he has milk and cereal in his hair.

He has a firm playdate with the twins lined up for tomorrow afternoon. Kathleen and I have a possible drive to Victoria lined up for tomorrow morning. If Tim is awake and out before 8:30 a.m.

then the Victoria trip is a go. If he is still sleeping I'll have to cancel with Kathleen.

Friday, March 24, 2017

We didn't get to Victoria. Tim rolled out of bed at 3:10 p.m.

I said, "I was on the verge of coming to wake you. The twins will be waiting at 4:30."

He was furious because I was presenting him with a problem "before he had a chance to put his brain in gear."

He was right; I shouldn't have mentioned the twins until he had been awake for a while. Like many people with an FASD, Tim has unusual difficulty shifting from one context to another.

He stayed angry while he got himself fed and dressed and packed. Then he said, "I'm not going down to that office."

I asked, "Shouldn't you be putting your boys first?"

Tim said the best thing he could do for his sons was *not* go to see them; he was going to go and buy heroin instead, and it would be my fault when he died. But he put a lot of fruit and pop and cheese sandwiches and cookies into his backpack, evidently planning to eat first and die later.

I asked him what was keeping him so grumpy and he said, "Everything!"

Nice. Mad at his life and taking it out on whoever is there. Likely as not, he will simmer down and go to his little guys. The fruit and cookies will be an adequate snack.

Wednesday, April 5, 2017

Saw the ophthalmologist in Victoria, as arranged one year ago.

My doctor here thought laser surgery might be possible to straighten my bad eye. But the Victoria specialist is not in favour of doing this and she has my total agreement. Surgery would merely improve the eye's appearance; it wouldn't be beneficial in any other way. From then on, I would need an eye patch to drive or walk or read or work because, with surgery, I would be seeing double—permanently.

Been there, done that. I remember the double vision following my first eye surgery. I remember walking on a slant out into the road and my mother grabbing my arm and pulling me back onto the sidewalk.

The vision tests today were standard: study a row of symbols and say which ones had been raised. (The whole row was absolutely flat.) Read the letters on the chart. (A good memory is helpful, here.) Watch the car and wave your hand when it goes into the garage. (It never got there.)

Kathleen came with me and she was wonderful. She is a super navigator. She stayed patient when we had to wait on the highway for a slowpoke at the top of the mountain to cut down a tree. While I was being put through every eye test in the book, Kathleen went and found a McDonald's we could walk to—and she had her 'free' coupons with her! I felt remarkably well cared for.

Monday, April 10, 2017
...and this would have been my forty-eighth wedding anniversary. Is it still an anniversary when only half of a couple is left to celebrate?

Woocher and I went out to Mountain Side Kennel this morning. He's booked in for two days and he loves being there. Lots of room to play, lots of company, and a big pond in the middle of the field.

When he first went to Mountain Side, he hadn't been with me for very long and he was overly friendly and sociable with everybody there. But now, with a well established owner and home, he understands he is temporarily at the kennel.

There are two reasons for Woocher to be at Mountain Side.

My hip has to have a break from his pulling; he is getting to be a bit much for me to exercise regularly. Kathleen bought a new type of harness for Pooh and he doesn't pull when he is wearing it. I'm going to try one on Woocher.

The other reason for using the kennel this week: my crawl space is packed with Tim's unorganized, half full boxes and I want to do a regrouping and check for dead food, dirty clothes, and drug supplies. But this is going to be a long, slow job and I don't want Tim to catch me in the act. Without the dog and his barking, I won't have to answer the door if Tim comes while I'm working. He says he can tell by the bark if I'm at home or if Woocher is alone in the house. This way he'll conclude we are both out.

Thursday, April 13, 2017
Supervisor B just sent me a very strange email. I've kept it because *somebody's* elevator isn't going to the top floor.

She wrote, "Tim's ex-girlfriend has heard from the managing director of the homeless shelter. They are looking for Tim, to offer him their services."

Supervisor B wondered if she could help in any way. She thought if Tim could get hooked up with the folks at the shelter, and if he was able to follow through, they might get him into supported housing.

She finished with, "I don't want to impose myself, but to help, if possible. Let me know if you would like me to follow up with the director."

My first question: Why on earth would the people at the shelter be phoning the ex-girlfriend?

She is on record as being "terrified" of Tim and has made it clear she doesn't want any official connection with him. How would the people at the shelter even know her name?

And why would the shelter be "looking for Tim?"

He is well known at the shelter, familiar with all the officials who run the place and already using most of their services. He is there several days a week. The folks in charge can talk to him at any point without the rest of us being included. And it's easy to get a message onto the jungle drums. If the shelter staff wanted him, they could have him there in thirty minutes, maybe less.

There is no question Tim needs and deserves supported housing and it should be through the government; it was their alcohol that caused his brain damage! But since he has trouble cooperating with a flexible and accepting mother, I doubt if he could cooperate with another rule-bound administration.

Sunday, April 16, 2017
Easter Day

I didn't get to early mass. The Easter vigil, last night, was lovely but I had to take a painkiller at midnight and slept through my alarm. Woocher needed to be fed and walked; by then it was too late to go back to the church for the morning service.

Kathleen and Tim were coming for an Easter lunch, or so I thought, but Tim came early needing coffee, a shower, and clean clothes. He had a dinner invitation for a friend's housewarming and didn't plan to come back for a noon meal.

Kathleen went to church. She has no car, so she walked all the way from home (without Pooh) and came in afterwards expecting me to sort out the rest of her day. We went to her apartment to get Pooh, had an early lunch at my house and watched one of her movies, and then I drove her to her friend's home for an Easter dinner.

Currently I'm appreciating an extended coffee and chocolate break while dog-sitting two restless beasts who are waiting for their suppers. The friend will bring Kathleen back here when her feast is finished. We will do a short, late stroll with our dogs before I take her home.

Friday, April 28, 2017

I had planned to help with a church function at 5 p.m. but didn't get there.

Tim showed up here at 3:30, stoned out of his mind and looking for a meal. He had a friend with him—they were holding each other upright. Tim was very polite, probably because he wanted to look good in front of Lyle.

When they had finished eating and were settled outside, with tools and bike parts and Coke cans spread across my lawn, and my door was locked and Woocher and I could finally leave, it was already 4:30. And Dog needs a nice long run off leash.

Monday, May 8, 2017
Another overdose. Tim came in early this morning with a hospital bracelet on his wrist. This is so horribly unpredictable. He was at the end of a good week and pleased with himself because of eight days with minimal heroin.

At least he was willing to talk. I heard every detail he remembered about his overdosing episode and he shared the kindly remarks made to him by the first responders.

He talked about rehabilitation but admitted he is afraid to go. I guess he would rather take a chance on dying than be alive and face the unknown. He is sleeping it off upstairs.

His belongings are getting emptied out of here, slowly, and mostly being passed on to friends and acquaintances. He understands my need of his room for the summer, but he isn't concentrating on alternative housing for himself. He is only making rehousing decisions related to his overflow of possessions.

He said, "My pathetic possessions."

For a street person, he sure owns a lot of stuff.

Tuesday, May 9, 2017
One of Tim's adult support team from North Island region has offered to take him on a tour of their local addictions treatment facility. She can arrange an appointment for him to view the place.

She said, "If Tim did the tour he might find the courage to attend. He needs longer than the six week program they offer but this could be a start. It might move him a tiny bit closer to rehabilitation." She is willing to do all the driving.

This might help—and we couldn't make Tim's life any worse.

Organization would be the problem. Coping with Tim is like working with quicksilver. The trick is to pick him up from his most recent institution and immediately take him where we want him to go with no input from him. And whatever we could work out would have to be free; he is costing the team an ample amount already.

He has a family doctor, although she seldom sees him. She would cooperate with a referral if we ever get that far.

Sunday, May 14, 2017
Mother's Day

Never a favourite of mine, although it was OK when my children were little. They had fun.

My childhood was blessed with the love and kindness of unmarried aunts; two were my mother's older sisters and two more were great aunts on my father's side. Let's remember those special women who mother without the necessary biology. Let's make it Mothering Day instead of Mother's Day.

This is Peter's birthday; he would have been seventy-nine. And Alex, my youngest son, died fifteen years ago tomorrow. For me there is only one pleasurable date in the middle of May—one of Zan and Bedelia's kids has a birthday this week.

Friday, May 19, 2017
Tim had a fight with his friend Chad, who threw a shovel and then a knife. The shovel caught Tim in the back: the knife handle hit his elbow.

He seemed to have recovered except for the worst part: being banned from the food bank for a week for fighting. But on Wednesday he arrived here with severe chest pain.

I suggested a doctor. "No way!" I drove him to his playdate with the boys, instead. He stayed with me overnight.

By Thursday he was ready to go to the walk-in clinic. Their web page said, "Open 8:30 a.m. to 5 p.m." I left Tim at the clinic at 8:30

a.m. and promised to return shortly but when I went back to see what he needed to do next, he wasn't there. They hadn't bothered to open until a few moments before 9. Idiots.

I made Tim an appointment for 10:20 in case he went back later, but he didn't.

He showed up here last night, with less pain as long as he didn't move or cough, and in an acceptable frame of mind. He wouldn't eat anything. He asked me to make him another clinic appointment. Haven't heard from him since.

I don't understand why he would be having such severe chest pain after a back blow; hopefully he got to the doctor and found out.

Sunday, May 21, 2017

Tim's shovel injury has been making him feel horribly ill. Today, in the middle of the long weekend, he decided he needed to see a doctor *right now*. We went to Emergency this morning at 10:30 a.m. and got back home at 3 p.m.

They did x-rays and an ECG. For the rest of the time it was just waiting. I did part of my waiting over a quick lunch at my cousin's cottage. Poor Tim had to sit for the whole stretch—mostly leaning against the wall or my shoulder. He didn't want to eat but managed to finish off a six pack of pop.

He has pneumonia and a cracked rib.
He has an antibiotic and gel caps for pain.

The doctor said he wasn't concerned about the rib; it is healing nicely and he could see from the x-ray Tim has had several fractured ribs in the past.

I said, "Starting when he was five," but the doctor told me early breaks don't show on adult x-rays.

However, the pneumonia needs special care. The old doc said he had some concerns, and he told me what to watch for. I will try to stretch the pain pills because the moment Tim feels better he will depart, and too bad if the antibiotics aren't finished.

This evening I sent an appeal to James for a solution to a problem. I need his help with locks and keys. James knows about locks; he has a friend who is a locksmith and they often work together.

Last winter an extra house key was hidden on my patio. (I thought.) Don't know when it vanished but there's no doubt Tim removed it and lost it. Or he might have sold it for drugs, although I haven't had a break in. In any case, a change of locks will be a smart move. I'm hoping James can tell me the quickest way to get this done and the most proficient local person to hire.

Wednesday, May 24, 2017

It's 8:30 p.m. and Tim just left on his bicycle. No doubt he has gone on a drug search.

My fault. He was struggling with a cough—part of the pneumonia—but it was too sore to cough because of the rib. I gave him half of a pain pill. The moment he didn't hurt, he vanished. I should have known! At least he had three full days of healing time.

The same setback would have happened if they had kept him in the hospital. No point trying to help this man through his predicaments.

Sunday, May 28, 2017

I am worn out and, at this moment, exceedingly tired of mothering a man with drug addictions, much as I love him. This has been a bad weekend. Calls from police officers; calls from the homeless shelter; calls from one of my neighbours. Alex's silver wolf necklace has disappeared from my bedroom, and there's no doubt the proceeds have gone to a dealer. I expect more of my goods and chattels to turn up missing.

Have to head up to the hospital.

Tim just phoned from Emergency; he has OD'd twice since I last saw him, probably thanks to Alex's silver wolf necklace. He told me he is going to rehab. (Yeah, right.) And he asked for smokes and an apple. I said I would come, bearing gifts, after walking the dog.

But then I changed my mind and will check in on Tim immediately, bringing Kathleen and two dogs. With no extra room in the car he can't slip out and get a ride to town.

Monday, May 29, 2017

Tim's immediate future appears to be a bit more hopeful.

He told me, "They're sending me to detox."

Not sure of the process, but the hospital is keeping him and that's a first. As a rule, he gets stabilized in Emergency and immediately sent off to use again.

He phoned last night and again this forenoon asking for something to eat. Apparently hospital fare is appalling when compared to the food bank or the Breakfast Club or spaghetti blah at the homeless shelter.

James and his friend the locksmith came and attended to my locks. There are replacements on the front door and the door opening into the garage. They have established new locks on two bedroom doors and the en suite bathroom.

Not that there is much left to steal! My pearl necklace and our gold wedding rings—the matching set Peter and I had specially made for our fortieth anniversary—have walked. And unlucky Kathleen made the mistake of leaving her silver jewelry with me for "safety."

I specifically wanted a lock on the front upstairs bedroom. It needs a deep cleaning. Keeping Tim out of there will give me a chance to scrub and get it back to being an appealing guest room for the rest of my kids.

The nights are warm now and Tim can sleep outside on my patio. It'll be comfortable. There's a brand new lounger for him, fitting in under the gable. A blue bin with a tight lid holds blankets, pillows, a light nylon quilt and plastic sheeting to cover if we are having a wet night. Another bin (bright red) has extra jackets, shoes and changes of clothing. A third bin (dark green) is for tools and bicycle parts. And there's a little bit of visibility on the patio throughout the night because of the street light at the corner.

Tuesday, May 30, 2017

Tim is still in the hospital; they want him to stay there until a detox bed opens.

When reminded of Tim's FASD, his nurses were vague. Apparently this bit of information, extremely important in my mind, hadn't been shared around.

I did my usual spiel: "This is a person with brain damage; intelligent but not always able to connect the dots. He has trouble understanding some abstract concepts like patience and feelings. His memory is intermittent. Please don't expect him to manage changes easily."

You can tell them a million times, but all you get back is, "He has to be responsible."

Sorry. He is unable, not unwilling, to be responsible. If he could somehow have been invested with responsibility and impulse control and reasoning ability he wouldn't have become addicted to drugs. I rest my case.

The nurse said, "We can't stop him if he decides to leave."

I already knew that.

Tim had an IV running yesterday, and there is an intravenous needle still stuck in his arm. I said, "Are they planning to drip another bottle into you later on?"

Tim said, "They left it there to make sure I don't walk out."

He is supposed to see his kids on Friday. Missed last week due to the pneumonia; will have to miss again this week due to hospitalization. Supervisors want to have a twenty-four hour warning and a reason if either parent has to cancel. Without the official warning the paying person on Tim's Team is charged the full amount.

The ex-girlfriend, although disallowing visits whenever she can find a good excuse, always remembers to cancel in advance. Tim has never called off a visit. He misses or attends as it suits him in the present moment.

If I get stuck with doing a cancellation, Supervisor B will be told nothing except, "He is still sick."

Tim told me he doesn't want his ex to find out he is in the hospital. She would be there instantly in drama mode. She would be crying, disrupting, questioning, and telling everybody how to take care of him and what an awful person he is.

Tim's probation officer called; he was trying to find his "most elusive client."

I said, "You can talk to him at the hospital. He's in Emergency, although he might have escaped by now."

The PO phoned again a while later to tell me, "Tim hasn't absconded yet."

Last weekend just before Tim was admitted to the hospital I found, strewn across my patio, large size men's clothes, small size women's clothes, children's clothes, tools, backpacks, and used needles. And, *following* Tim's admission, an empty Coke can.

I don't care who owns any of it. The whole lot has gone to the strata garbage container.

Tim had an extra single bed as part of his mess in the upstairs bedroom. It occupied vast amounts of space and blocked a window; we had to perpetually fight our way around the box spring. He was keeping it "for his new apartment."

There is nothing to rent in the whole town.

I told him the bed had to go but it didn't. At last James and I (mostly James) hauled the wretched thing downstairs and out onto the patio.

I asked Tim, "What do you intend to do with your bed?"

He said, "It can go to the dump."

Not, "I will get it to the dump." The removal has become my problem. Bruce promised to help. The bed is presently covered with a tarp and being rained on.

My doorbell doesn't ring anymore. A smart friend suggested dismantling the innards and another friend did the deed.

Tim has complied with most of Mom's Rules but even with the clock on the windowsill he totally ignored "Mom's Hours." The doorbell rang at *all* hours, specifically middle-of-the-night hours, and was accompanied by deep, loud, excited barking. Woocher knew it was his friend, Tim, outside. And there I was, wide awake and having to make a decision: answer it? … or ignore it.

Knocking is better. When a knock wakes me up it isn't such a jolt to the nerves. The dog recognizes Tim's bang on the door; he mutters to himself but doesn't bark. He understands Tim will walk around to the patio. And for me, going back to sleep is much easier after a knock.

Wednesday, May 31, 2017

Tim has disappeared from the hospital.

I went up early with breakfast treats for him and found his bed empty. And somehow the room *felt* empty.

The ward clerk at the desk said, "Isn't he eating his breakfast?" He wasn't—we went and had another look.

It never pays to get hopeful where Tim is concerned but this is particularly distressing. The medical folks certainly did try. If only a detox bed had come up before heroin enticed him.

There is a note on my front door: "Hi Tim. You have to see Basil. He wants to talk to you before I welcome you in."

There is also a bag hanging on my doorknob; the breakfast treats he missed out on earlier.

Thursday, June 1, 2017

Tim showed up here yesterday at noon. He had already been to the probation officer and had proof in writing—one of Basil's business cards with the date and time of the next appointment. When I told him his visit with the boys had been cancelled, he was furious. No reasoning, no acknowledgement of the twenty-four hour warning, nothing but an overabundance of bad temper.

I said, "Change it. I said you were still sick; you can phone and say you are much better." But it was a lot easier to get mad at me.

Right on cue the phone rang; it was Supervisor B. I don't know what she planned to say to me because I put Tim on before he could escape. They talked (peacefully) and organized for the usual interaction at her office at 5:30 p.m.

Then Tim, in quite a different state of mind, said, "The twins' birthday is coming up. We can have an early party. Could you get cupcakes?"

Those cupcakes! I tried at Superstore since I was there anyway for my regular shopping. No cupcakes. I got a yellow cake decorated with little flowers, in case nothing more promising could be found.

Then a quick stop at Save On. They had chocolate cupcakes with coloured sprinkles, prepackaged and gooey. I got some of those on the chance nothing more exciting was available.

And at last out to Thrifty's—my least favourite grocery store. They had beautiful cupcakes designed for birthdays, and the baker boxed them in separate little containers with a cardboard ring to keep each one upright. She even gave me a free package of candles.

And gifts! I had already bought two gift certificates from the local toy store. We wrote on them: from Oma and Daddy.

Kathleen had organized two bubble blowing kits and two cards; they were at my house in gift bags.

James had brought me a box of nearly new binders for the church bazaar. They had sticky labels on the front, which came off easily using alcohol swabs from Tim's harm reduction kits. The result was two shiny new red binders; I filled them with coloured paper and stickers and a card—"From Uncle James and Aunty Elaine." I'll have to remember to warn Elaine in case there are "thank you" calls.

And I will have to phone Bedelia with the same warning. She and Zan had given me a bag of colourful little cars and trucks, several nearly new, their kids had outgrown. Originally intended for the church bazaar, the best of these now became birthday gifts.

For months, Tim had stored a package of children's lanyards in my carport. I found them buried underneath his winter shirts. There were two designs: some with whistles attached and others with tiny working flashlights. The dollar store provided zippered cases decorated with a Canada flag, big enough to hold two lanyards. One whistle and one flashlight for each twin.

With getting everything organized and tagged and gift-bagged I was late at the supervisor's office. Tim and his youngsters were already established. Knowing the ex-girlfriend's rules—No family; No friends; No photos—I expected to be stopped at the door but Supervisor B said, "Ruth! Come in!" I got to hug the twins and catch up on their preschool and daycare news while Tim doled out cards and parcels and the cupcakes.

It won't hurt any for Supervisor B to realize Tim has a big family behind him, with every one of us missing his children.

I have to remember to put money into the church bazaar envelope!

Saturday, June 3, 2017

Tim is once more talking about detox. He went to Drug and Alcohol on his own and came back with a handful of pamphlets. But he was stoned again today.

He has dealt with his latest warrant. It wasn't a big deal. He was subpoenaed to be a witness for a circumstance he couldn't remember. Since he had no idea what it was all about, he ignored the whole problem. A warrant was issued. He didn't bother with his summons, either.

When the police officers apprehended him, he told me, "I didn't run. It was too hot." He said the officer had thanked him for not running.

I met one of the officers in the off leash park. He stopped to talk to Woocher and informed me, "Tim is all caught up."

Tuesday, June 6, 2017

Kathleen and Woocher have the same allergies. They are both confronting cottonwood this week. Kathleen is wheezing and Woocher's eyes are a mess.

Tim's room is empty. I'm going to get a professional company to clean the carpet; it's covered with ground-in food and spilled pop and dried blood. He has already used the patio lounger and found it comfortable: another hurdle jumped. He has made his peace with Jill at the food bank. He is no longer tolerated inside Superstore.

My bedroom door has been kept locked for years. Like many mothers of kids with FASD, I have always worn the bedroom key on a chain around my neck.

Now that the door between the en suite bathroom and my walk-in closet remains permanently locked, many of the things that used to vanish have found a secure home. Batteries, household tools, Scotch tape, nail clippers, flashlights, wooden spoons, WD-40 and toilet paper live on the closet shelves. Also, oddly enough, the lens cleaner for my glasses. A giant box of Q-tips is tucked away, and I take from it to refill much smaller boxes in the bathrooms.

My mother would have been 105 this week if she hadn't escaped.

Thursday, June 15, 2017

Kathleen and I were walking our dogs at the back end of the park. As we trudged up the long hill, a silly woman passed us on her bicycle, travelling downwards at top speed and yelling to her dogs to keep up. The dogs, barking wildly, chose the quickest route directly through each of the walking groups on the hill. Pooh joined in the chase and Woocher, in his new harness, managed three steps—just sufficient to jerk me to the ground.

It is embarrassing to fall in public.

I went down on my left hip, the one with bursitis in it. But the worst result of this crash is a sprained ankle. Can't figure out how my right ankle got hurt since it was on the wrong side.

Sunday, June 18, 2017

A doctor who works in Emergency phoned my number and asked for Tim.

I said, "Tim doesn't live here. I'm his mother."

The doctor asked, "Will you be seeing him soon?"

I said, "Possibly. He comes and goes."

The doctor laughed. "Like a feather in the wind. Can you give him a message?"

"It depends on the message." Being a volunteer secretary, I don't feel compelled to pass on information.

Tim had blood work done during his last admission for overdose and this doctor had paid attention to past records. He told me Tim needed to make an appointment with his family doctor. "As soon as possible."

I asked, "What has he got? Hep C?"

"I'm not able to say," the doctor reminded me. "Privacy Act."

I said, "He is talking about going to detox and rehab, and while there is a chance of those happening, I'm not going to tell him any difficult news," and, "You do understand my son is functioning at a fourteen-year-old level while he's using?"

The doctor agreed, with, "Oh yes. And I can tell you have been around this bush before."

At the end of the conversation he tucked in, "You are an accomplished guesser."

I saw Tim, but I didn't tell him about the doctor's phone call.

One reason: he would be instantly angry (at me) and any emotional distress leads him into more substance abuse.

Another reason: he might use this as an excuse to avoid rehab. And if he needed to be on a course of antivirals, would rehab even take him?

The third reason: getting him to go to any doctor is usually an exercise in futility. There would be no point in trying until I knew she had seen his blood test results.

Thursday, June 22, 2017

One of my friends on Tim's Team did some Hep C research.

"Doctors might be willing to put off treatment. Sometimes it clears up without help. The medications are new and expensive so Pharmacare may not pay for it anyway, until there is liver damage."

She thinks it might be better to wait until Tim is through detox, and already into rehabilitation treatment before I pass on the message.

She said, "My feeling is 'go with your gut' because your gut has been doing this for a long time."

Another member of Tim's Team put in the necessary effort to organize a tour at the North Island Rehabilitation Centre.

Tim was supposed to be here at 7 a.m. for breakfast and a shower. The team member was supposed to pick him up at 7:45 for the tour at 10. And I got up at 6 a.m. to get Woocher's walk and breakfast out of the way early.

Tim didn't come. Yesterday was Welfare Wednesday. I guess the Thursday after Welfare Wednesday was not the best date to plan a tour.

Friday, June 23, 2017

Supervisor B just sent me an email: Could I provide her with Tim's most recent Notice of Assessment? She wrote, "I understand this was part of the mediated agreement."

I haven't got any Notice of Assessment. I don't even know what a Notice of Assessment is, but it will be legal and connected to money if the ex-girlfriend is interested. And it can't be anything to do with treaty annuities because Skye has already organized for Tim's Band money to go to the twins instead of to him. His Band money is supposed to be his child support.

Skye talked about getting the paperwork regarding his income across town to the ex's lawyer. I thought that was done.

And why is Supervisor B asking for this? Is it on behalf of the ex-girlfriend? I know the ex insists upon long, detailed discussions with each supervisor after every playdate; maybe Supervisor B is trying to keep those communications as smooth as possible. But I don't think finding documents is part of her role.

I'm not impressed with the way the second mediation is working out, although it seemed better while it was going on. There were a lot of "future plans" in the mediated agreement but where is the follow-up? The ex-girlfriend is eager to have her rights acknowledged. What about Tim's rights?

But there's no question I am the only one concerned with this kind of unfairness. For Tim, any problem that arises is automatically his own fault because of his drug use.

Haven't seen him for ages. A bad sign.

Saturday, June 24, 2017

Notice of Assessment—Got it! You have to file your income tax to get this. If Tim qualifies for the standard seventy-five dollar rebate, sent to most folks on disability, the Notice of Assessment will be attached to the cheque. I wonder if the seventy-five dollars is what the ex-girlfriend is looking for?...or if she just wants control of his affairs?

Sent an email back to Supervisor B to tell her I can't provide Tim's Notice of Assessment and have no notion of where it could be but will mention it next time I see him.

He showed up late this evening, hungry and cheerful. He said the supervisor should be asking him, not me, if she wants any of his private papers. Perfect!

Saturday, July 1, 2017

Tim is so thin. He must have dropped one hundred pounds in the last eighteen months—maybe more. He gets lots of exercise; he is always walking or riding his bike. But I don't think he bothers to eat unless he is here with me.

Heroin seems to take away a person's appetite. Most of Tim's street friends are skin over bone.

Company for supper tonight. Tim brought along a young guy named Douglas, who looked about twelve but said he was nineteen. When I opened the door, this lad offered a polite hello, ran across the kitchen and threw up in my sink. He was most apologetic. Tim said he had been bullied at the river camp.

Saturday, July 8, 2017

Woocher hurt his back leg while he was working on his rock pile out in the middle of the river. X-rays indicate a ruptured cruciate, in a knee already weakened with a touch of arthritis. Surgery has been suggested—for $5000. Surgery will not be happening.

There are veterinarians who do dog therapy and massage and ultrasound. My vet has given me two dog therapists to contact, to see what they can offer. (One would come to Woocher at home.) She said either of those could get treatment started and then teach me the exercises. Our hope is to stabilize the knee.

Woocher has a new pain medication but he couldn't be started on it at once because the half aspirin I gave him had to wear off. The new pain tablets work: he is much less restless.

I got a sliding pet ramp for him to use getting in and out of the car, since he's not supposed to jump. At first he backed off and wouldn't try it. I bribed him with peanut butter smeared on the ramp. He went up the slope and into the car without even noticing. My dog will do anything for food.

Monday, July 10, 2017

A new dilemma is giving me the creeping jeebies but it doesn't bother Woocher: when he walks his knee clunks with each step. Or is it your elbow when you are a dog?

What a gruesome sound! His walking isn't any different; it's the same limp as before. Why do these complications always choose to happen on a weekend?

I had already organized with the new therapist before this clunking began. She is coming to my house tomorrow for an appointment that will cost $200 + GST. Much more affordable than $5000 for surgery! She said she is opposed to surgery in almost every case. This vet and Woocher's primary vet collaborate and she will study his x-rays before she comes.

Sunday, July 16, 2017

We came safely through another overdose. This time, Tim didn't even bother to tell me about it. I found two wet plastic wristbands, both with Wednesday's date, lying in the bathtub and a new list of prescriptions crumpled beside the bathroom sink.

A few days later he told me about his latest paramedic who had said, "Any allergies?"

Tim had replied, "Heroin, apparently."

The paramedic, liking Tim's sense of humour, wrote "Heroin" on an allergy bracelet and clipped it onto his arm along with his official ID.

Tuesday, July 25, 2017

There is a new dry out center, a little room around the back of the homeless shelter. Not sure who pays for it but Tim seems to be using it quite often.

He said, "I can go there when I'm under the influence, any time of the day or night and sleep for twelve hours." Sounds just like home. He especially likes one of the older nurses, Helen, who works there.

Thursday, August 10, 2017

A delightful week in Calgary with Cricket and Clay and my grandchildren. We had mild weather with sun and clouds and occasional soft rain. I came back to disagreeable heat and thick smoke from forest fires across the province. We are being promised rain on the weekend. It would be well received. There's been no rain here for six weeks.

There are boxes of apples in my hallway and life ahead will be filled with applesauce. Cousin Elizabeth has a huge, overgrown yellow transparent tree. The apples make lovely sauce but they don't keep, and we both feel guilty if they rot. We'll be spending the next while in our kitchens, peeling and coring and cooking and freezing and drying.

Tim was involved in an accident while I was in Calgary and it had to happen when he was on his way to the water park for a supervised playtime with his sons. A lady, opening her car door as he rode past, knocked him off his bike. He came to in the middle of the road with a crowd standing around, one of whom was an off-duty firefighter.

The firefighter checked him over and thought Tim was in shock, with a possible broken collarbone. That was because the last broken clavicle, never x-rayed or braced, has left him with a sagging shoulder. Somebody dialed 911, but Tim was sure he was fine and refused the ambulance.

He went to the nearest safe place, planning to wash and recover before seeing the boys. He woke up six hours later. Too bad about *that* visit.

Woocher did well at the kennel, except he chewed his harness in two and I had to buy him a new one. Forty dollars and worth every penny because it stops him from pulling.

He is getting eight fifteen minute walks daily. With walking and with the ice pack on his leg three times a day, and with the exercises the travelling vet taught us, his leg has stopped clunking but he is still limping and still needing pain pills.

Sunday, August 27, 2017

The Diocese Family Camp was fun and I'm glad I could go. Zan and Bedelia were both tremendously busy and the older kids were mostly involved with their own programs. I got to have the youngest for long stretches during the days.

This camp is for the whole island. Families from my own church were there, and friends I remembered from last year. I was one of the oldest at the camp. My cane was a real asset; without it I couldn't have kept up with a lively two-year-old travelling from sand box to trampoline to playhouse to rocking horse to swings to slide.

Zan and Bedelia, being workers as well as campers, had to stay until the last scrap of paper was picked up and the last tablecloth was washed. We didn't get back to my house until 6 o'clock this evening and they had a further long drive to Victoria still in front of them.

Haven't seen Tim. Hope he isn't in custody but at least he would be safe.

Too bad I can't collect Woocher from the kennel until tomorrow morning. My feet are sore from four days of walking and Woocher has our ice pack.

Wednesday, August 30, 2017

On Monday morning Tim presented himself, hoping for breakfast. He told me Jay was coming too, and bringing his puppy. Jay had nowhere to leave the pup. They thought I wouldn't mind since I am fond of dogs.

Baby Tiger is a ten-week-old, absolutely adorable pit bull cross. His ears meet at the top of his head. He peed enormously on my living room floor, bless his little heart. Woocher was patient; he only growled once when Baby Tiger hauled on his tail.

I am trying to get photos of all Tim's friends when they come here for meals. If they overdose and die, there will at least be a memory. Jay didn't want to pose, with or without his puppy, but he cooperated when I offered to take a second picture of Baby Tiger by himself. He was thrilled when I promised him a copy of both photos.

Late on Monday, I came home to find Tim's bike in my flowers and a body at the far edge of the lawn. It was Tim, his face grey, lying mostly on the road.

I said "Tim!" but there was no response. I touched his hand; it was cold. But at my touch he woke up, instantaneously and with vigour.

He hollered, "You scared me!" He had no clue, at first, where he was or how he got there.

He has a dreadful bruise on his forehead, a black eye, and a swollen wrist. We suppose he must have fallen off his bike and hit his head.

I wish he would stop operating that bloody bike when he's using drugs—he is so tippy and riding is so dangerous. He has a bad headache and ringing ears.

All I feel is tired.

Thursday, August 31, 2017

An answer to the letter I sent to the Minister of Justice and Attorney General of Canada! I am thrilled: Jody Wilson Raybould is somebody I admire enormously. Her letter is glued into my journal because it's from Jody and also because I want to keep track of any promises made by the Liberals.

Dear Ruth:

In reference to your correspondence concerning Bill C235, An Act to amend the Criminal Code and the Corrections and Conditional Release Act (fetal alcohol spectrum disorder)

I appreciate the effort you have made to share your personal story and views on this issue. Please accept my sympathy for the difficulties you and your son have experienced.

As you may know, Bill C235 was introduced into the House of Commons by Member of Parliament the Honourable Larry Bagnell on February 25, 2016. Since it is a Private Member's Bill, it was debated in accordance with the rules of Parliament for Private Members' Business. This legislation was defeated at Second Reading in the House of Commons on December 13, 2016.

However, please be assured our government is aware that fetal alcohol spectrum disorder (FASD), like other disorders and mental illnesses, presents a challenge for the criminal justice system. I am committed to conducting a review of the changes in our criminal justice system and sentencing reforms made over the past decade to address gaps in services to those with mental illness. As part of this comprehensive review, I will consider those with FASD and other mental disorders and cognitive disabilities.

Respectfully,

The Honourable Jody Wilson-Raybould, P.C., Q.C., M.P.

Minister of Justice and Attorney General of Canada

Friday, September 1, 2017

Supervisor B sent a note. Once school starts, she wants Tim's interactions with his sons extended: 5:30 p.m. until 8:30 p.m.

I'm having a bit of trouble with this. It's an awfully long stretch, and 8:30 p.m. is too late for little kids to be dealing with emotional upheavals. I'm *not* directing their bedtimes! Wouldn't the ex-girlfriend love to pin "interference!" on me? But I do think they should be out of there by 7:30 at the latest; they need to settle down before they sleep.

I'm not sure Tim could hold it together for such a long stretch, either. Some days yes, other days no. In my opinion, two hours is adequate. Also, anything more would be mighty expensive for the member of Tim's Team who pays.

The complication—and there is always one of those: Supervisor B wrote in her report the boys love being with Daddy and wish their playtimes could be longer.

We had a strata meeting tonight. I was late, as Tim had to be sent back to his camp before I could leave. But it was okay—the other owners had seen his bike on their way past and they knew I couldn't leave my house as long as he was in it.

Sunday, September 3, 2017

Tim's friend, Red, is back in town: trouble with a capital T. He has been in Alberta for the last fifteen years and I sure hope he returns there. Soon. Red's traumatic brain injury happened because of an accident when he was five.

He stole cars and trucks with Tim back in the early nineties; they also did their breaking and entering together. Red's criminal record is even longer than Tim's. Hate to remember the countless hours I've already spent in court with those two. Red is the friend who pushed Tim at the top of a flight of stairs and caused one of his worst compound fractures.

But now Red has decided to be The Helper. He asked me, "How

long has he been this way?" and assured Tim, "We will get your life straightened out." I'm not holding my breath.

Tim came in for supper on his way down from a high, most likely heroin. He did mutterings about Red; I therefore assumed Red would be joining us and when he appeared he had Rachael with him. It was my first meeting with this particular Rachael although Tim has produced two others.

Mostly, the kids need either direction or help when it comes to cutting cheese for their buns, but this Rachael knows how to use a cheese slicer. Her father is Dutch.

Monday, September 4, 2017

Zan thinks it's "cool" that I've had fifteen years without Red in my life.

He said, "If Tim and Red get back into the break and enter scene, it may not last as long as it did twenty years ago. Tim will be easier to catch since age has slowed him down."

And a sensible email from Supervisor B—the visits will be from 5 p.m. until 7 p.m.

Friday, September 22, 2017

Tim has missed another visit with his sons.

I had an unpleasant email from Supervisor B; she is demanding his reasons for not coming.

Why ask me? I have nothing to offer as to why he didn't get there. Does it matter? He didn't get there. I do feel badly for the children and for Tim's Team who have to pay, regardless, when this happens.

Anyway, it's up to Tim, not me, to give to all those interested an explanation of why he wasn't there.

The ex-girlfriend and I met accidentally in town this morning. She allowed the twins to greet me. Now I see why. She already knew I was going to be reprimanded by Supervisor B.

Although my support of Tim is expected by everybody, I have been unavailable to him for most of this week. We are holding the annual bazaar at our church, a huge, six day proceeding for which I have major responsibilities. My son does less well whenever I'm not helping him right out front.

Also, part of the problem here is Welfare Wednesdays. I suspect, without having any proof, the ex-girlfriend insisted on Wednesday visits chiefly to sideswipe Tim. My opinion: Visits scheduled on Welfare days should automatically be cancelled. He would be ticked off, but too bad. He's the one who messes up and he isn't paying.

There are times when it appears as if being with his kids is not helping. I wonder if supporting these playdates is enabling? ... or if the playdates are keeping him from going completely over the edge? I don't want an answer to this question.

Thursday, September 28, 2017

Tim is in jail.

He was scheduled to attend in court. I went too, as we had planned to organize his Legal Aid immediately following the appearance. Stefano had already promised to represent Tim and had told him to ask for another undertaking in three weeks. But Tim was grabbed by the arm while we waited in Courtroom Four and was arrested for multiple thefts before he could appear in front of the judge.

It is not a joy seeing your son handcuffed. At least I got to give him a hug.

Tim phoned from Duncan courthouse cells (one call permitted) and asked me to bail him out. I told him I couldn't afford to do so. For ten years there had been an envelope of money in my top drawer marked, "$500.00 for Tim's next bail."

I said to Tim, "The envelope has vanished."

He said, "Your drug addicted son stole it."

He told me he expected to be sent to the Regional Correctional Centre on Wilkinson Road in Victoria. I promised to notify James and Elaine, as they live in the same district and can more easily arrange to see him.

Then another telephoned request, this time from the court sheriff, asking me to come back to the courthouse and discuss Tim's bail with the duty counsel.

Duty Counsel was a stranger to me, an agreeable young chap who wanted to be helpful. He thought the best plan for Tim would be to first pay the bail and then work on getting him into detox and rehab.

Does he imagine we haven't tried???

I said, "Detox and rehab will happen if they are court ordered. Is this something you can arrange?"

Evidently not unless the arrest is for addiction. Theft to assist addiction doesn't count.

Then our less than self effacing Administrative Crown Counsel stepped in. He had a lot to say, most of it disagreeable. Tim had already been through *five* apprehensions at one store and had *five* charges of theft from the same store. Crown had asked for $500 bail because he wasn't learning from these mistakes.

Surprise!! When have our folks with FASD *ever* learned from their own mistakes? They can't. Their brain damage attends to that.

If Tim's bail was paid, said the Top Crown, he would go back to the same store, steal again, be arrested again, be charged again, and the bail money would go into the system. Nothing would change.

"If, on the other hand, he goes to jail, everybody, including Tim (and his mother who looks as if she needed it) will get a break and a chance to rethink. Maybe some changes will happen."

Although the duty counsel was trying to help Tim, I agreed with the Administrative Crown Counsel. His comments were well reasoned and sensible.

I took several moments to explain to both of them, in as much detail as they had patience to hear, that Tim had been born with brain damage. His difficulties, while being made much worse by heroin, were not *caused* by heroin. Therefore, he needed a court ordered plan of action, court ordered rehabilitation for about ten years and court ordered supervised housing following rehab. That got a laugh.

My government is not prepared to provide for my son's needs—he looks too good and sounds too good. I wish he looked as compromised as he assuredly is. Then expectations would be a lot more realistic.

At our parents' support group meetings, many years ago, we used to wish our kids born with FASD had also been born with fluorescent blue hair.

Monday, October 2, 2017
Tim had a rough detox at Wilkinson Road Correctional and in the end he got sent to Victoria General Hospital. The wardens thought he was having a heart attack.

He phoned to tell me he is over the worst but still being held in the medical section of the jail for observation. He hopes to go from incarceration to rehabilitation as soon as possible. He expects court will be on October 10 and he plans to plead guilty and get the wheels of justice rolling.

He has started the application for Legal Aid. He wants Stefano and he is hoping his team will supply rehab suggestions. Last week it was a "might" and a "maybe." Today he started the conversation with, "Can you guys get me into rehab?"

I'd say he's as committed as he'll ever be.

Tim said he feels more human than he has for ages but his body is crying out for extra sugar. He has been approved for the weekly canteen. His Christmas money—now divided equally into twelve monthly portions—is due this week. I will phone Wilkie and find out if they will accept a cheque via snail mail. Even if they say, "Yes," money sent to the person in charge at the jail always takes ages to get through. Maybe James or Elaine could drop off a twenty to keep him going until I can get my end organized.

Family and friends, and even lawyers and probation officers, have to phone to make visiting or drop-off arrangements and their calls have to be during business hours.

Thursday, October 3, 2017

Tim phoned again today. He is still in the medical wing. Wilkie's lines rattle terribly, and Tim, as his father before him, doesn't appreciate being asked to repeat. I'm guessing at details but this is the gist.

His court date is definitely October 10. He has got his Legal Aid organized. He is assuming the team will offer suggestions for rehab. He is assuming the judge will buy into the team's optimal choice. He is assuming, if rehab starts early, he will get out of jail early. Probably none of these assumptions are correct.

I've talked to Stefano and he has officially become Tim's lawyer. The team can contact him anytime between now and Friday evening, but he'll be unavailable for the following week. He's trying to either organize a duty counsel for October 10 or get the court date put forward to October 17.

Nobody is willing to guess how much time Crown Counsel will be asking for. But Stefano said, "If Crown wants two months Tim wouldn't be getting out anyway. A court date a week later won't make any difference."

Meanwhile, Tim's brain is circling a mile a minute as he tries to think of somewhere to stay between jail and rehab. This is his usual FASD perseveration: he is unable, not unwilling, to move on.

I'm hoping there won't be a space between jail and rehab! A prison term is not guaranteed to be clean and sober but there is more chance of success inside than outside.

Wednesday, October 4, 2017

I will be going to see Tim on Thanksgiving Weekend. Mary Grace offered to drive and I accepted with pleasure; it'll be super to have somebody along to share the burden. For me, there are no warm memories of Wilkie. Every other penitentiary was easier to visit.

Our visit starts at 2:40 p.m. but we have to be there at 2:10. They said it takes thirty minutes to sign in and you have to bring two pieces of ID. The same as flying to Calgary! There won't be guards with guns standing behind us while we visit. I asked.

Nowadays, family members are not permitted to bring anything to inmates. Twenty years ago when each correctional facility had its own rules, I could usually hand across photos and notes from siblings and crayon drawings from little cousins, and I could share a hug with Tim above the divider when it was time to go.

In one jail, ice cold tins of Pepsi could be purchased from a pop machine. The guards had to open the cans; then you and your convict could drink together separated by a metal screen.

In another (it might have been Nanaimo) there was a big visiting room, free coffee and tea, and little tables set around. Families were playing board games or cards.

At New Haven, in Burnaby, which was my very favourite correctional center, bar none, we brought an open box bulging with socks and soap and shampoo and deodorant and games and magazines. The whole package was passed to the wardens. They handed it across to Tim, right in front of us, with *no* inspection.

But I will never forget my very first experience of an adult prison. We didn't know anything about their rules and never thought to ask, assuming everything would be the same there as it had been in juvie. It was Easter Day. We confidently produced our gift for Tim, a big tin of homemade sugar cookies. Little yellow ducks, brightly coloured eggs, pink and blue rabbits, and white swans, all iced and hand decorated. He wasn't permitted to have them; we had to take the whole lot back home.

Friday, October 6, 2017
Bedelia left a message on my answering machine. Zan wants to visit Tim, and they wondered if Zan and I could go in together. He had hoped to go with James, but James is on day shift and booked solid for the next week. Mary Grace said she would give her spot to

Zan and come with me next time. Hopefully the jail will accept the change.

James went in after work to drop off spending money for Tim, but he was too late; they close the front desk at 4 p.m. He will be able to go earlier if he can regroup his service schedule. And I won't be allowed to leave money as the front desk is behind bars on weekends.

When Tim was in the medical wing, he was phoning me frequently. Back in the general population, he's not calling nearly so often. I send three letters for every one coming back to me because I want my son to hear from his family as often as possible.

We are hoping he can go to rehab directly from prison. His probation officer, and his team, and Supervisor B, and the family are all in touch with the lawyer, asking for immediate rehabilitation. I even went and talked to the official enemy—Crown Counsel.

October 9, 2017

Thanksgiving Weekend

What a pleasant fifty-five minutes with Tim!

Zan and I waited off to the side of the main visiting area in a little booth. Two sides were partitions, the back was open to a wide hallway where, behind us, guards walked back and forth, and the front was floor to ceiling glass. We had two chairs on our side and a two way telephone.

Tim appeared abruptly on the other side of our glass. He was delighted to have company, pleased to see me, and positively thrilled Zan had come too.

Tim had his phone all to himself, but on our side of the glass communication had to be shared. When Zan held our phone I could see Tim's mouth moving but I couldn't hear him. Tim had a lot to say; Zan worked out a way for us to listen simultaneously.

Tim plans to plead guilty tomorrow. He told us there is only one way to get from this prison to rehab: go to a halfway house for two weeks. The problem is there is seldom a room available at the halfway house exactly when it is needed.

Stefano said he was going to check in with Crown before he left last Friday since he can't be there tomorrow. Between them, they may have decided to put Tim forward a week. On the other hand, as this case is pretty clear cut, they might use the duty counsel. Tim won't hear what's happening until breakfast.

Thursday, October 12, 2017
Tim had his court appearance on Tuesday and it was a gong show.

The lawyer already knew he couldn't be there and had arranged with Crown Counsel for a week's extension. But Tim's name hadn't been removed from the court lists, so the correctional facility sent him to the courthouse in their van.

The office of the Crown, besides messing up the court lists, hadn't regrouped with the duty counsel. Duty had a fit when he heard he was expected to represent Tim; there were already twenty on his list.

He told me, apologetically, "You might as well find something else to do until later."

But it was before 9:30 a.m. and most businesses in town were still closed. I stayed in the main courtroom.

Then Tim's ex-girlfriend waltzed in, with a huge, gloating grin pasted on her face. She is unique: the only person I have ever seen steadily smiling in a courtroom. Everybody else appears to be either terrified or absolutely miserable.

Why she thinks she has to lose a morning's work and sit in court is anybody's guess. Usually the extra people who come along without being on trial are there to support.

I saw the ex from across the way. But one of Tim's Team caught her in action a while later, when she was leaving the courtroom with a lawyer. She was pestering him with questions and he was angrily telling her not to talk to him in court. If that fellow is going to be her lawyer in the future then Tim will be fortunate; he's not sensational.

One of the Crown Counsels for Tuesday was the Administrative Crown who had advised me against posting bail for Tim. He watched the ex-girlfriend come back into the courtroom with her smile in place. Then he glanced at me, handed over to the lesser Crown, and bowed himself out. A while later, I decided to take a short break. I didn't want to miss Tim's turn but sitting there watching defeated people getting nothing in the way of help or support is draining.

The Administrative Crown Counsel, busy with his note pad and pen, was sitting on a chair outside the courtroom door. He didn't look up. But the duty counsel came rushing across the hall and told me he had just heard from Tim's lawyer. (Doubtful. I think he had just heard from the Top Crown.) He said it would be in everyone's best interest to postpone Tim's hearing for a week. He mentioned something about "private" that I missed. Early in the day there is constant noise and commotion in the courthouse corridors.

But I'm remembering Tim's last hearing, put forward twice, and the pugnacious ex furious about *her* time being wasted. And in the end they used a little back room without the ex knowing anything about it.

Anyway, there was no hope of seeing Tim and therefore no reason to stay.

Friday, October 13, 2017

Tim called twice this afternoon.

First he had news to share: his hearing will be this coming Tuesday and it will probably be videoed at the jail. He isn't thrilled; he prefers a change of scene.

In my opinion, the Administrative Crown Counsel has worked smoothly and amazingly quickly to arrange with lawyer, judge, and jail in order to keep his office free of the ex-girlfriend. And they really are paying attention to Tim's needs in spite of the way they usually muddle through.

Tim's second call was a request, long and complicated. He has been doing his usual wheeling and dealing, and this was about having me cheat the system and put his monthly Christmas money into someone else's account. I didn't pay any attention. He can work his money problems out for himself—he has lots of leisure time!

Monday, October 16, 2017

Stefano phoned me, long distance. His car has conked out in southern Manitoba and the duty counsel will be acting for him tomorrow.

He said Legal Aid hasn't sent him Tim's contract. So far, he has only a spoken agreement: without something in writing he won't get paid. But he *has* got a secretary—not sure why this is my responsibility.

I phoned the Legal Aid office and got put on hold for twenty minutes. It was worth the wait; I ended up with a woman who said she was new and seemed anxious about being accurate.

She said, "We can't give out any information."

I said, "I don't *want* any information. I only need you to send the contract to the lawyer, Stefano Esposito, and then he can act for my son, Timothy Spencer."

She said she would send it right away. Fantastic!

Later on, I heard from a man at a different Legal Aid office in a different town. He wants Tim to phone him.

He said, "When I have heard from Tim, I will be able to get the case lined up for tomorrow without Mr. Esposito."

Why involve me? I have no way of reaching Tim. I can only leave a message that he will get "within twenty-four hours." Why can't this official phone the prison *himself* and sort it out?

I was polite.

But what a system! Not only does the left hand not have a clue what the right hand is doing, those two hands aren't even connected to the same body!

Stefano phoned this evening, from Saskatchewan. He has been authorized as Tim's lawyer and said he is pleased to take this on, as Tim has so much support.

Tuesday, October 17, 2017
    Zan just phoned. Tim had been taken to the main court in Victoria early this morning, had finished his hearing, and was now free.
    The guards had told him he could either find his own way home or he could go back to Wilkie and let the folks there sort it out. That would have taken an extra day (not Tim's way of doing things) so he got himself dropped off in downtown Victoria and walked to Zan's office.
    Zan said, "He is wearing the prison uniform—a light grey jumpsuit and *bright* orange crocks. You can't miss him!"
    Zan had given him enough money for the up-island bus and for food at McDonald's.

Wednesday, October 18, 2017
    Tim got home last night. He had supper with me, shared stories about life in the slammer, showered, changed into his own clothes and shoes, and left his usual mess in the upstairs bathroom. It was a pleasure being with the real, drug free Tim.
    Firstly, he is supposed to see his probation officer this morning. Secondly, he intends to go to the shelter and organize a bed. Thirdly, he'll stop at Drug and Alcohol; he has firm plans for rehab. My fingers are crossed.

Sunday, October 22, 2017
    My project for today was to cook the turkey we didn't eat last Christmas.
    The necessary ingredients were prepared, ready to make stuffing, but when the defrosted bird was unwrapped it was already stuffed. This was a new experience for me and a bit tricky, as I was slightly doubtful about the turkey's condition. One hot day during the summer Tim had left the freezer door not quite closed. The freezer lives in the garage and I didn't chance upon his mistake until the next day.

The bird needed to be cooked for six hours, which seemed to me excessively long, but the company who stuffed it ought to know.

When it had seventy minutes still to go, Tim came in with Ethan. (Tim and Cory had joined me for breakfast.) Tim and Ethan thought a turkey dinner would be "awesome." I hadn't counted on the dinner part but tinned cranberry sauce was easy. I made a salad and Tim defrosted buns. The gravy was already there because of it being that kind of a turkey.

We were smart to eat an hour early; that bird was close to being overdone and mostly stuffing—two kinds. And it was oddly shaped. The wishbone was long and narrow.

Between the three of us we managed to shatter my mother's teapot. Aunty Sheila's teapot is unbroken, of course. I never liked it.

Ethan burned his arm and I pronged the back of my hand.

Monday, October 23, 2017 and it's 11:20 p.m.

Tim presented himself at my door half an hour ago, distraught and shaking. He might have been hit by a car and knocked off his bike. He is in a lot of pain but can't remember much and the missing memory is bothering him no end. He has used something—but not heroin; this isn't his usual heroin reaction.

Anyway, he is bedded down on my patio and hopefully will sleep through the night and leave early. I don't want to see his wounds and then get shot down for suggesting a doctor.

Wednesday, October 25, 2017

Tim came in with two problems.

Disability benefits are suspended for prisoners who are incarcerated for more than a month. He wasn't in custody that long, but his cheque has gone missing. He will have to go from office to office and possibly make a trip to Victoria trying to get his affairs sorted out. There is supposed to be a playtime with his sons today, but he might have to miss it because of his money worries.

He arrived here in a rotten temper. From his general attitude, I suspected he had used already and since I'm not putting up with rudeness anymore he didn't get instant sympathy.

I said, "I'm sorry you are having money problems, and I'll help if I can. But you need to calm down. Either be polite or leave."

He left in less than sixty seconds, in a worse temper than ever and with pop from the fridge. On the way out he told me he wasn't going to the visit; he was going to do drugs instead and it would be my fault.

Not. But I do find these emotional ups and downs wearing.

Thursday, October 26, 2017

James phoned this morning. He wanted to know if the money he had taken to "the stockade" had been spent or if Tim had been released before junk food day?

He asked, "Should I drop by and inquire? … or would they just mail that to your address?"

It would be sensible to at least find out what the procedure is. Tim left clothes and shoes behind and he will let them sit there forever. The clothes aren't worth bothering about but the shoes are his newest pair.

Friday, October 27, 2017

Tim dropped by yesterday at suppertime for a wash and some food. Neither of us mentioned my ultimatum of the day before. He was bright and cheerful and probably high, although sometimes it's hard to tell.

Haven't seen him today and I hope he doesn't come in now; we are past "Mom's Time."

We have a family function—Zan's birthday party—tomorrow in Victoria. Tim might join in. I said if he decided to come he should be in front of my garage at 9:30 a.m. or at Kathleen's back entrance at 9:45.

Sunday, October 29, 2017

It's 1:10 a.m. on Sunday. Just back from a long, intense hospital session followed by a cold, wet dog walk. Sleep is far, far away.

Tim came to my house this evening at about 8 p.m. with a hugely swollen, agonizingly painful hand. He said he came for "a little bit of mom time" and then he was going to ride his bike up to Emergency. I drove him there, instead.

At the hospital they did blood work and put him on an IV full of pain killers and antibiotics, and did more blood work, and sent him off for an x-ray and to pee in a pot, and did more blood work, and told him they wanted him to stay for the night because his kidneys are shutting down. They wanted to keep the fluids going in, keep the painkillers going in, and keep ice packs on his hand. Tim refused to stay.

He said, "This whole place is too much like jail."

He wouldn't come to me, either. He has gone to his tent. This is Tim's lack of reasoning ability showing up again; it is *not* 'being stubborn.'

He has to go back for another IV tonight. And he has to come here in the morning for his new pills. Before he comes, I will have to get myself into town to organize his new pills.

When he handed me Tim's prescription, the doctor said, "I'm not pleased your son is going against medical advice."

Neither was I.

Still Sunday, October 29

Tim came in for his meds. He said if they offered a bed tonight he would happily take it. He isn't peeing much and seems to have a chest condition getting started.

The hand doesn't look any different and the pain is excruciating, but he won't take over the counter analgesics. Ever since his very first overdose—Tylenol, at age eighteen—he has been terrified to swallow ordinary painkillers. And yet he injects heroin directly into his veins.

Lynn is hanging around; she is truly concerned. Kathleen keeps calling from home and crying.

Monday, October 30, 2017

I was blessed with Kathleen and Pooh this morning, and Lynn for most of the day. She didn't leave until Tim and I were ready to go to the hospital at 8 p.m. She said she was going to her grandmother's for the night.

I said, "Then why are you taking sandwiches along?" because she had made herself a large bread and cheese meal. Grandma, it appears, won't feed anybody who is 'late' and she won't let Lynn loose in her kitchen, ever.

Lynn knows her way around *my* kitchen and she zips through, taking care of her own needs. She also cleans up after herself.

Tim has remembered to come, two days in a row, for his morning pill. The hand looks terrible but he showed me he is able to clench his fist. As usual he tried on multiple sets of clothes and left them where he dropped them, throughout the house. But as he puts on his long-sleeved shirts he groans and moans and whimpers.

Every so often I wish Peter, instead of me, had been stuck with this upheaval. The ideal is to *not* be left behind either as widow *or* as widower. Ever since my brother-in-law died and his wife was too desolated to cope with the work death involves, I've known it is preferable to be the one who dies first.

Still Monday, October 30

Tim and I had a session at the hospital again tonight, and he got another IV bag full of medications pumped into his healthy arm. He also had a second series of tests. The results show an improvement in his kidney function with a lower pulse rate, lower blood pressure, and a lower white cell count.

The hand is more swollen (I wouldn't have thought that was

possible!) and flaming red, with long dark lines going up his arm but tonight he can move his fingers.

He will be getting another IV tomorrow night.

I would say the situation is improving, except he has gone back to his tent where he can add expensive illegal drugs to the free mix. Too bad because if he had come here an ice pack might have helped.

Wednesday, November 1, 2017

This was Tim's fifth night of having a bag of antibiotics and etc. dripped into his arm. Tonight, a nurse carried an IV pole out into the waiting room and hooked him up in front of everybody. It was much more interesting for Tim; several street friends were there and he didn't complain once.

He can wiggle his fingers a bit more, and the hand doesn't hurt if he doesn't move it or bump it.

A doctor wanted to see him before we left; an extra thirty minute wait but marvellous news. Tomorrow morning he can try for an appointment at the IV clinic downtown. If he can get in there, during the day, we can quit with these 8 p.m. until 11 p.m. episodes.

However, I'll stay as involved as possible for as long as possible because once the pain stops, Tim will quit going. Even though he is suffering it has been tricky to keep him attending at the hospital and cooperating with the staff.

And transportation is a matter of me planning ahead and Tim not working things through. With his bike locked into either my car or my house, he can't leave the hospital unless he walks.

Tim's oral antibiotics are living at my house and he is supposed to take one at breakfast and another at supper. We have both forgotten the supper one twice.

We had Halloween callers, last night, but Woocher made unfriendly noises on our side of the front door and the small clowns and witches scuttled off. Then Tim and Seth came in for supper, having knocked on the patio door. Woocher was beside himself with delight. Friends at last! Seth ate and ran because he wanted to keep an eye on Tim's tent.

Friday, November 3, 2017

Tim managed five trips to the hospital five nights in a row with a lot of support, bribery, and trickery on my part. And most mornings he has shown up for his medications. But on Thursday he was supposed to go to the IV clinic for his first drip. It *would* be during a day when I was completely tied up. Without my underpinning, Tim didn't get there.

He came in for supper and his pill last night (still Thursday) and he could have gone up to the hospital for an IV but he wouldn't budge. He said he was due at the clinic on Friday, scarcely twelve hours later, and since he had taken his pill he would be fine.

We got to the IV clinic at 11 a.m., as arranged, and the nurse there told us we had come at the wrong time. Tim's appointment was for 1 p.m. She had scheduled it herself.

Well, I was involved with the scheduling and it was for 11, but as James always says, "Just smile and nod." Smiling worked. The nurse said they had extra staff on and could do Tim straightaway. And best of all, at the clinic IVs run for twenty minutes instead of being six times as long.

Tim has to be checked by his family doctor next week. They can't go on pumping antibiotics into him forever; someone has to say when to stop. But Tim's doctor has her office at Superstore and Tim isn't allowed to go inside. I had to find the manager and make arrangements to get Tim through the store.

We worked out a way to manage that part but then got bogged down at the doctor's office. First problem: Tim has missed two appointments and is no longer on the approved list. Second problem: He will have to come in as a walk-in patient and wait until somebody can check his hand. Tim is a patient without patience; I suspect he won't bother to wait, especially if the pain is less.

And more bad news, this time on the local radio station. The homeless camp above the river got raided by the RCMP operating in the dark on the coldest night of the year. They confiscated tents, bedding and blankets, boots and shoes, extra clothes, flashlights and bikes: if it was loose on the ground they took it. And there was Tim, out in the cold with a badly infected hand.

Haven't seen him since the raid. He has probably found a couch and won't be in for his meds. Hope he shows at the IV clinic tomorrow.

Saturday, November 11, 2017

Tim's lab work has improved, although the hand looks ugly. He had his last treatment on Tuesday when he saw a doctor at the IV clinic. And that after all my efforts to get him to his own doctor at Superstore.

The new doctor has shifted Tim to oral meds. These new pills are supposed to be taken at six hour intervals and Tim isn't able to manage so much responsibility. As he left the clinic he dropped his prescription; thankfully he was still in the parking lot. Somebody found it and brought it back inside. The clinic called me. I went and got the prescription and had it filled. So far, Tim has taken six pills; he should have had sixteen at this point.

The destitute, who were camping in the bush and got raided by the RCMP, have shifted to a vacant lot across the street from the homeless shelter. Tim is there; he managed to rescue his tent and bike. The new camp made the front page of the local paper. The authorities want the campers out of there without delay but the owner of the property has gone missing and so nobody is asking for this tent city to be removed. I hope the owner stays lost until next March.

Tim hasn't seen his sons since he last went to prison. The ex-girlfriend has cancelled all connections until rehab has been completed. The lawyer and others involved in Tim's affairs also believe rehab should come first. But the twins want to see their daddy and at the moment their daddy isn't thinking in terms of rehabilitation.

Monday, November 13, 2017
A letter from Skye this morning. Tim isn't in any condition to absorb the contents right now. Best to save it until his situation improves—if it ever does.

Hi Ruth:
While Tim is using, and his health is bad, it doesn't surprise me that his ex has suspended visits, even though they *are* supervised.

Do you think visiting can wait until Tim has gone to rehab and he's been clean for a while? If Tim, himself, chose to suspend access and put new parameters in place while he's sick, it would show the judge he doesn't want to submit his kids to his disease at its worst.

He could ask that the twins are taken to family gatherings. And he could get letters or cards together to send the boys once in a while, for instance, telling them he loves them, misses them, and when his health improves he'll be seeing them.

He could fight for maintaining his supervised visits, but if he's not healthy enough and has to keep cancelling, that will reflect badly upon him. He needs to make substantial, lengthy efforts to convince a judge he will maintain his access. Judges are not happy when parents see their children, and then disappear, and get lost in time.

Thursday, November 16, 2017
Kathleen, Tim and I had lunch at The Good Neighbour to celebrate two birthdays. Kathleen will be forty-eight this week, and Tim had his birthday a few days ago. He came to the feast late and left early but at least he was there. And he certainly ate his share.

Wednesday, November 22, 2017

Tim is missing the playdates with his sons but I don't expect there will be any changes. He appears unconcerned about rehab; he is merely marking time. Skye will come on board as his family lawyer the moment he needs her but he isn't moving in that direction either.

He is still dropping in on me frequently for a wash and clean clothes and a meal. He routinely brings a bag of dirty laundry. My friends tell me Tim is the cleanest street person on record.

Usually he is high, reasonably polite, and friendly. Yesterday he needed a fix and was absolutely horrid but today is Welfare Wednesday. I won't be seeing him. I mention the twins at every opportunity, but there isn't much apparent interest.

He is handling a triple whammy. Getting back onto heroin following the prison detox, plus having such an appalling infection in his hand, plus the police raid—these have joined forces to cause major changes in his emotional stability.

No suggestions where to go from here, short of kidnapping him and putting him on a sailing ship for ten years as a deck hand.

Monday, December 4, 2017

We celebrated St. Nicholaas yesterday and when the guests had departed I became aware of how badly my memory has slipped. I forgot to pay Bedelia for the Norwex products she brought me. I forgot to reimburse James for Tim's expenses in jail. I forgot to give Mary Grace a box of trinkets for the next church bazaar. I forgot to ask Elaine to get me more Splenda at Costco. I forgot to turn off the coffee perk.

Worst of all—I forgot the truffles!! They were buried in the fridge underneath Woocher's fresh carrots and I never thought of them until my company had gone home.

This morning Tim was discovered sleeping on my patio. He said he had been there most of the night. I didn't hear him arrive and

Woocher didn't growl. The lounger is comfortable; he was warm and dry in spite of the weather. What a relief this is working out!

Tim drank a cup of coffee and has been resting on the couch ever since. I don't think he is ill, as he keeps rising up to get himself more to eat.

I will deliver bags of St. Nicholaas treats and chocolate letters for the twins when Tim has gone on his way. The doorknob of their other grandparents' house will be a most appropriate spot for a hanging.

Monday, December 11, 2017

Got blessed with Tim this morning, along with Charlie and Miles; none were stoned and all were polite. They cleaned out my banana supply and were hard on the cereal and heavy on the pop—for breakfast!

I had made a Christmas card for Tim's boys. Santa and a snowman riding on an antique tractor, totally appropriate for a father to give his sons. Tim wrote a Christmas message inside it, and we sent it through the mail to Grandpa's house. He'll make sure the kids get it.

I have a horrible cold. Couldn't possibly be flu because I had a flu shot. But it has been pretending to be flu ever since Saturday when I walked out of church in the middle of the service feeling light-headed. The chilly outside air helped.

Walking Woocher twice a day is the most I can manage right now. You could *make* a dog with all the black hair I haven't vacuumed off this floor!

Friday, December 15, 2017

Tim and I went down to Wilkinson Road Correctional; he needed to get the shoes, clothes, and money he had left there. The money should go back to James. It won't.

Tim finally got moving on this, shortly before the deadline. If you leave belongings longer than three months the jail steps in and your stuff is gone forever.

But this was a filthy day for driving over Malahat Mountain, what with rain and heavy fog and Christmas traffic. My germs came too, and so did Tim's leg cramps. It was quite a trip.

Sunday, December 17, 2017

My cold is improving. However, there is another health complication and it makes me feel as if I'm about to faint—especially in church. This is a blood pressure related problem I've dealt with before: vasovagel syncope.

Will make an appointment with my doctor when she is back from Hawaii, just for a checkup. No point going to her replacement as this disease has recognizable triggers and I found out, years ago, what to do for it. Lots of fluids, extra salt, don't stand still for a long stretch, keep lifting your feet.

Mary Grace suggested, "Sit at the back of the church."

Splendid advice: from there it's easier to get out without a big production. Moving about and fresh air both help.

Tuesday, December 19, 2017

Tim has a bed in the Courtenay Rehabilitation Centre and he is due to start there on Wednesday, December 20.

He just told me he is also supposed to appear in court on December 20. That's tomorrow! I gather he has one more theft charge with a risk of incarceration. He isn't coming unglued at the thought of another term of detention and he hasn't bothered to inform his criminal lawyer. I did that.

Still Tuesday.

Stefano phoned. He said it has been more than three months; Tim will have to apply for Legal Aid. He is taking cases in our area again, so he can help, but the problem is he can't be there on December 20 because he has court in Victoria. But if Tim can go in on his own and adjourn for three weeks, Stefano could take over on the next court appearance.

Feels as though we are going in circles here regarding Wednesday's schedule. I put a list on the patio door for Tim, and another on the kitchen door for me:

a) Ask for an adjournment in court.

b) Go to Legal Aid after court because their office is open only on Wednesdays.

c) Keep the appointment with the probation officer.

d) Get back to Mom's place in time to catch your ride to Courtenay.

Not sure if any of this will happen.

I went to the Crown Counsel's office because Tim has a pink slip that is supposed to get Legal Aid moving faster, but the man I needed to talk to has been shifted to Victoria. However, the Administrative Crown, who is well acquainted with us, was there. He said they could get Tim through quickly tomorrow morning; he already knew rehab is supposed to start in the afternoon. He told me "we" have another court date in January.

And the people in Courtenay phoned. They are aware of Tim's medical issues; hopefully they will also deal with any court dates while they have him.

Tim's probation finished last month, and there is no longer any reason for the ex-girlfriend to be told when he is arrested and charged. But she hears from someone, somehow. I wonder if Stefano is the person who could close this gap? Tim's privacy is being infringed upon and Kathleen is finding the Triumphant Ex a bit irritating when she comes to the slum to buy her marijuana.

Thursday, December 21, 2017

Tim was supposed to head up island yesterday at 2 p.m. with one of the nurses from Drug and Alcohol. They have been exceptionally supportive.

And he was supposed to come to my house in the early afternoon to leave his bike and get his clothes. He didn't come here, but he might have gone north. Or he might have chickened out at the last moment. Unfortunately, it was Welfare Wednesday; his money goes into his account at 6 a.m. and then he does two days of aggressive spending. If he is in town, I won't be seeing him.

Sure hope the court saw him.

A Christmas note from Zan's office was fun. He signed it, "Yours in work-place-appropriate seasonal merriment."

Friday, December 22, 2017
Tim didn't get to rehab. Not a surprise, with the trip planned for Welfare Wednesday. He is interested in going and he might have made it the day before.

I didn't see him on Wednesday or Thursday but he was back in Emergency last night. Another overdose—the heroin was from a bad batch laced with fentanyl. He phoned, wanting me to bring his shoes. I had poppy seed cakes in the oven and promised to be there eventually, but he sorted himself out and arrived here just as the cakes were finished.

Although he had overdosed at the homeless shelter, where no drugs are tolerated, he was planning to go back there for the night. The managing director had given verbal permission.

I had heard the shelter officials have their favourites.

Tuesday, December 26, 2017
James and Elaine came up to Duncan on December 24. The week before they had invited Kathleen, Tim, and I to share a Christmas Eve lunch at Good Neighbour. The food was fantastic!

Afterwards, James decided to put up more of my Christmas lights. They sparkle in layers all around the outside of the patio. I'm trying to remember to switch 'on' when it gets dark and 'off' at bedtime. Sure hope James comes back to take them down.

Cricket phoned on Christmas Day all the way from an extended family get-together in Florida. She couldn't talk for long as there were ten children yelling in the pool beside her.

Kathleen had a nasty headache yesterday and no energy to get herself anywhere but Tim came very early for a bowl of cereal and to pick up his Christmas present. And now, with Tim having money in his pocket, I'm anxiously hearing every siren wailing past on the lower road.

Our power went out this morning but not for long. Imagine if that had happened yesterday with turkeys cooking in ovens all across town.

2018

Wednesday, January 3, 2018

Alana and Bruce always celebrate the beginning of the new year with an afternoon open house on January 1. This is a fun occasion for three generations of extended family, plus a profusion of friends. And since most of my family gathers at Uncle Bruce's, those who can stay longer come to my home for supper.

Tim dropped in on me before the open house, in satisfactory condition, but then he went back to his camp instead of going to Uncle Bruce's gathering. When he showed up for the family function he was stoned and silent. He slept on the living room couch for the whole evening.

Oh well, we are into a new year. Onwards and upwards.

Friday, January 12, 2018

Tim's latest court date was Tuesday, January 9, but I didn't know about it until Stefano phoned me that morning. What an obliging man. He will carry on being Tim's lawyer if the Legal Aid paperwork ever gets signed, but for now he is staying in touch without being paid.

Tim had missed his own trial. Crown had just warned Stefano a warrant would be issued at 6 p.m. unless Tim got himself down to the court house and personally organized a new court date for two or three weeks ahead.

And Legal Aid has to be lined up. Stefano can't do much until he is officially retained.

Before Stefano phoned, Tim, for the first time in a year, had cooked himself two eggs for breakfast instead of eating cold cereal.

He was positive the police were chasing him with a warrant. He had been keeping out of sight and neither organizing Legal Aid, nor checking in with his probation officer, nor asking at the court registry office for the date of his next appearance.

I got a big hug and a last goodbye in case the officers caught up with him. Haven't seen him since. After hearing from Stefano, I put a note on the patio door and went out searching but I didn't find Tim. He might have come past and seen the note: he might have dealt with his issues.

There were two big drug busts in town on Tuesday night, both at previously condemned houses where Tim hangs out. Since then, Tim hasn't been seen. He could be in difficulties or in jail. I hope jail.

Sunday, January 14, 2018

Tim has surfaced.

He was not in either crack house when they were raided, and hadn't been arrested, but he knew every detail of what had happened.

There is now an official warrant out for him. He is hiding from the police and comes here in the dark. As far as I'm aware, he hasn't sorted out his Legal Aid, hasn't seen his probation officer, and hasn't contacted the drug and alcohol folks regarding another try at detox and rehab.

Wednesday, January 17, 2018

Kathleen called to tell me she is worried.

On the way back from the park, she and Pooh met Tim's ex-girlfriend, who was just leaving Kathleen's apartment building with a package of marijuana in her hand and a huge smile on her face.

Thursday, January 18, 2018

Tim is back in jail. I hadn't seen him since last Monday. Finally made inquiries and there he was, in custody.

Last fall his detox was so bad they had to take him from the lock up to Victoria General Hospital. Hope it is easier for him this week. The staff will make him get cracking on his paperwork for Legal Aid as soon as he has detoxed.

Court will be here in town next Tuesday. I'll try to get to Crown Counsel before then to see if they can make compulsory rehab part of his sentence, just for a change.

Sunday, January 20, 2018

Back into "busy" mode. I got Tim's bathroom cleaned. It was a slum, up there. Now the walls and floor are washed, the skylight has been vacuumed, and all the soap and shampoo empties are gone.

This is what's nice about having a break from the drug scene:

Normally I don't begin any time-sensitive tasks such as baking bread or complicated tasks such as clearing out a cupboard, in case Tim arrives in rough condition. Not that I follow him around the house; it's just a matter of paying attention but everything else has to be put on hold for the duration. Now I'm able to finish a long chore without interesting interruptions.

And this is what's appealing about strata living:

One night last week my outside light burned out. I can't reach it; my little household ladder is too short. When I got home the next afternoon, my neighbour had put in a new bulb.

Monday, January 22, 2018

Tim called from the prison, feeling human for the first time since his arrest, but with every joint hurting. He has already completed the request to make Stefano his lawyer again. He has court tomorrow.

As usual, having suffered through detox, he is eager to go to rehab and wanting to come to me between jail and rehab. As usual, I'm hoping there won't be a gap between jail and rehab.

I'm also hoping Stefano can prevent an in-house stay, with my house being presented to the judge as an option. Conditional sentences are for young parents. I'm too old to deal with a bored and fed up son who wants out. And I'm *not* going to be the officer in charge.

But I could do it if they put an old style electronic monitor on him. Tim was hooked to one of those, very successfully, twenty years ago.

Stefano just phoned. He sure is working late!

He has received notice from Legal Aid regarding Tim's case and he will be there tomorrow. He promised to make sure my place is not advanced as a housing alternative.

He said, "I will enquire about rehab, but as you know, it takes a lot of organization."

Tuesday, January 23, 2018

Court this morning. It was just old theft charges waiting to be dealt with—nothing new or terribly bad.

Stefano was impressive. He played both the "FASD" card and the "Mother in Court" card.

The judge said, "Mr. Spencer. Do you know how often I see a mother? Especially for somebody your age? Almost never!" and, "When you make promises here, to me and to yourself, you are also making them to your mother. Do you understand?"

Tim said he did.

With a good lawyer and a personable judge, court wasn't as miserable as usual. I was acquainted with, and had fed, many of the folks waiting for trial. I got a big grin from Harry Peter and another from Percival George. Little Poppy was there, looking petrified. Whenever I see Poppy, with her soft blue eyes, I wish her mother had named her Violet.

This afternoon Tim phoned from Wilkie. He said, "You're recognized at court, Mom."

The sheriff had gone to the cells beforehand and had told Tim,

"Your mother is here. I don't think she has ever missed one of your trials."

For twenty five years. They tend to remember their regulars.

It'll be about a month of incarceration, this time, with part of the sentence already served. Tim is currently in Wilkie but he expects to be shifted to Brannen Lake Correctional Institution in Nanaimo.

He said, "Don't worry about coming to see me; I'll be locked up for barely a month," but I will go if I can.

He has already got a request in to see the Wilkinson Road Drug and Alcohol person. Probably the request, if not the person, will transfer with him to Brannen Lake. The team and the family are hoping (again) Tim will go from incarceration straight to rehabilitation.

I'm not particularly knowledgeable about the rules for visitors at Brannen Lake Correctional, but dropping in is never permitted, anywhere.

At Wilkie, an appointment has to be made more than a week in advance. You must arrive thirty minutes before your scheduled visit for sign in. You must put everything you own in a locker. Peter got himself into lots of trouble, back in 2001, because he kept his handkerchief in his pocket, pulling it out to blow his nose midway through our visit with Tim. Visits are exactly fifty-five minutes long and nobody can leave early unless removed by a guard.

Zan and I were privileged at Thanksgiving: we had that little booth with two-way phones. In the main room, there are guards standing at the back behind the visitors, watching the inmates. And it's a good thing. I remember a visitor who tried to climb over the metal separation screen to give her incarcerated boyfriend a kiss.

Looking forward to a month of ease apart from creditors, mostly personal finance companies, who have been given my telephone number thanks to Tim. Those companies hand money to people without ever checking their credit ratings. It's their own fault if folks don't pay.

James said, "Good news about a break for you, Mom, but sad for Tim. Don't pay any of his bills. Pass on his new address to the loan sharks. He will enjoy getting mail."

Wednesday, January 24, 2018

I expected the ex-girlfriend to be present in the courtroom yesterday for Tim's trial, but she wasn't there.

She had been at my place earlier that morning. Woocher and I were almost home after a wet walk when, to my amazement, she zipped around the corner and stopped her car.

She said, "I left a bag from the boys on your door knob. Sorry it took so long."

I gave her an enormous smile and a "Thank you," and she seemed grateful and a bit weepy.

It was then about 8:30 a.m. and I was sure I would see her in court at 9:30, but she didn't come. Tim's lawyer must have gotten the word out: no need for Tim's ex to be informed, as her issues were dealt with long ago.

Anyway, this is a fabulous excuse to connect by email and be admiring. The "Thank You" drawings from the twins, with their names in wobbly capitals, are lovely. Definitely a family endeavour.

For a simple email, it used up a lot of energy. Because I can't totally trust the ex I kept a copy, and have pasted it into my journal.

> Please tell the kids "thank you" for their beautiful cards. I'm familiar with how much effort it takes from mothers for these projects to happen!
> Tim had a court appearance yesterday, and he will be incarcerated until the last week of February. If you need a break, you are welcome to drop the boys off with me for a while. I have kept the train set, and a big box of cars and trucks, and there are new art supplies in the craft cupboard.
> Hoping to hear from you.

Tuesday, February 6, 2018

Tim has been relocated to Nanaimo, a much better situation than Victoria because the men are kept occupied. He says Wilkinson Road Correctional is "hard time;" there's nothing to do. But Brannen Lake has the unfortunate reputation of being a drug haven.

When Tim was in Wilkie, before Christmas, he checked in with me frequently and wanted to go to rehab. There have been very few calls from Brannen Lake, meaning he is happier, but when I mentioned the Courtenay Rehabilitation Centre he wasn't particularly interested. Hope he hasn't discovered a new drug supply.

If he is using, he will need to take double to cope with company. I'm not keen to go through the trouble of organizing a trip up island simply to find him high. Trying to decide what to do.

Wednesday, February 14, 2018

What a marvellous afternoon!! The twins and their mother came for a visit!!! I opened the door when they knocked and truly could not believe my eyes. Poor Woocher was speedily pushed into the garage; that was his contribution to peace in the family.

The children had created a gorgeous homemade valentine for me—mostly red foil and lace. It was carefully clipped onto the art screen in my kitchen before they went home.

I have a plastic bin full of 'survivors,' the last of the toys my own kids played with many years ago. In moments the twins had their old favourites strewn across the floor.

They remembered Oma's craft cupboard and were excited to find, along with the expected felt pens, paper, crayons, glue, and scissors, a box of beads and laces and a tin of glitter. Both little boys are keen on arts and crafts.

I offered coffee but the ex-girlfriend had brought her own, along with a big box of doughnut holes. We all shared those, and the kids had hot chocolate.

It was a successful visit, messy and merry, with no disturbing undercurrents. "Tim" was not mentioned, but we did talk about "Daddy."

The twins had lots of questions. I had given them an old fashioned photograph album at Christmas: pictures of themselves with Daddy and Mommy, and also with members of Daddy's immediate family. Fishing in the creek with Uncle James; blowing bubbles with Aunty Kathleen; riding in a wheelbarrow pushed by Uncle Zan; washing dishes with Oma; decorating a Christmas tree with their cousins; wearing dress ups with Aunty Elaine and Aunty Bedelia. They only remembered Oma, having seen me regularly at the pool with their Daddy and Supervisor A.

They stayed for an hour and a half! This was an opportunity I never thought would happen, ever.

Thursday, February 15, 2018

When I was driving through town, a car banged into the back of my car. Both drivers were doing less than the speed limit. At first I thought a bomb had exploded inside the car. Even small accidents are surprisingly noisy.

No one was hurt, but both drivers are about the same age (elderly) and were somewhat shaken up. Her front fender has a dent, and my back bumper has the imprint of her license plate, backwards.

We exchanged information. I got a claim number from ICBC but won't need to use it. Car and driver are both kosher.

Saturday, February 17, 2018

A call from Tim at last! He has been falling into bed the moment his day is over, too tired to think, never mind make phone calls. The prison inmates are repairing British Columbia's gigantic fire hoses and getting them ready for next summer's forest fires. Tim says he is having lots of fun being part of a team, but he had to get used to heavy labour.

He is taking a new drug and plans to make it permanent. He said while he is on suboxone he doesn't crave heroin, and any opioid he might use would make him incredibly sick. He has to see his doctor as soon as he gets home, and every day from then on he has to get the pill from the pharmacist and let it melt under his tongue, right there in the pharmacy.

If this works for him it might be a more sensible plan than rehab. We've been told rehab isn't particularly useful for people with brain damage who turn out to be unable, not unwilling, to make the necessary lifestyle changes. I don't have any stats for how well suboxone works for folks with an FASD.

Tim intends to go to AA meetings, book in at the homeless shelter, and not search out Lynn. He is working toward seeing his boys. Sure hope he can stick with it, as he will have money in his pocket when he leaves his correctional facility.

Tim has had five letters from me - and I have sent nine. We both realized, years ago, numbering letters going in and out of prisons is a wise move.

The twins' Valentine cards, which I had sent to their Daddy, were resealed and returned because they had done their drawings with wax crayon. If Daddy is incarcerated again they'll have to use pencil crayons. Wax crayon drawings aren't sanctioned—there might be drugs hidden under the wax.

This was a long collect call. We had lots of news to share and I did most of the talking and valued every minute of it. Tim was overjoyed to hear about my get together with his sons and his ex; he said such awesome news more than compensated for a month in lock up.

Monday, February 26, 2018

Tim is home and catching up on the mail he wasn't allowed to have during his incarceration. A bright flower sticker on the back?—not sanctioned! There might be drugs under the sticker. A missing return address?—not sanctioned! If they don't know who sent it, they won't let the inmate have it.

Sure is a pleasure having Tim around when he is sober. Unfortunately, his first appointment with a doctor here in town to get his prescription for suboxone filled isn't until Wednesday. Figures. But he has a friend who sells heroin and hands out suboxone and if he remembers he will ask her for a tablet to tide him over.

Thursday, March 1, 2018

Mary Grace and I went to Tofino for three relaxing days at Middle Beach Lodge. She organized everything; I had a wonderful holiday! No phones, no radio, no computer, no texting, no iPads, no news. We did watch a little bit of Olympic coverage on the TV provided by the management. Fantastic food. Long walks on the beach. Glorious weather.

Before Tofino, I went with Tim to meet his new doctor, the one somebody at the correctional facility had set up for him. He asked me to come. He hates anything different and he was so nervous that he was making me nervous. When we finally found the office, it turned out to be part of the overdose prevention site and totally familiar. Tim is already friendly with most of the professionals who work there and with all of the people addicted to drugs who use there.

Nearly twenty minutes of paperwork, just to sign in. We did it together—a good thing he wanted me to come along.

Tim's new doctor is Dr. Nguyen, a young, gorgeous woman, remarkably kind to both of us. She has increased his suboxone from twelve mg to sixteen mg and he has to see her in a week to decide if he needs more. She will try to get his blood work from the prison medical center so he doesn't have to go to the lab here in town and get poked again.

Saturday, March 10, 2018

Tim is still taking suboxone, and he is staying off heroin. He is using crystal meth instead. I see him almost daily but he has missed appointments with his new doctor and his probation officer.

There was a strata meeting tonight. With Tim off heroin and onto speed, I'm finding it easier to get him moving towards departure. He could hardly stand upright while I was easing him out the door but at least he stayed cheerful and fairly polite. He leaves more mess and muddle behind himself on speed than he ever did on heroin.

Friday, March 16, 2018

Elder College offered a course in estate planning, wills, representation agreements, power of attorney and choosing executors. I signed up for it. Because we collect more personal information every year and because the Estate Law changed in 2011, I'm needing to organize lots of paper and make a few financial changes.

It'll be necessary to get a safety deposit box at the credit union for house papers, my last will, and any jewelry Tim hasn't already stolen. The lawyer teaching the course suggests an accordion file, keeping all the information connected with estate, final illness, and funeral in one place and making sure the family knows where that place is.

I'm switching one account from collecting interest to collecting dividends, which will mean changes to my will. At the moment, this account is to be split five ways for my five kids, when I am deleted, with Alex's share going to his daughter.

My plan is to ask Mary Grace to be in charge of my health decisions, to ask James and Zan to both be Powers of Attorney but able to act separately, to keep James as Executor, since he doesn't have the added responsibility of children, and to ask Bedelia, Kathleen, and Elaine to empty out this house. I'm not expecting any of them to take on the support of Tim.

The lawyer suggests a family meeting while I'm still competent mentally. Then my kids will be enlightened (together) as to what I'm planning for both estate issues and end of life choices.

Wednesday, March 28, 2018

When I hadn't seen Tim since late last Wednesday, and I knew he had recently switched from speed to heroin, and I knew he had moved his tent for more privacy, I started to get anxious and finally called the RCMP.

They said, "Don't worry, he's not missing. We've got him."

Tim is back in the pen. Third round since Halloween.

Stefano said Tim had been charged with theft and breach. The trial had been last Thursday, first thing on the court agenda.

This didn't make sense to me. Between late on Wednesday when I had been with Tim, and early on Thursday when he was in custody, most of the stores would have been closed. Not that he wouldn't have taken an easy and convenient opportunity to steal, if it had presented itself when he was stressed, anxious, or high, but he was in good shape when he left my place and I didn't see how he would have had time for a theft.

I called the probation officer, who hadn't breached Tim and thanked me for telling him what was going on.

I called Wilkinson Road Jail to set a visit date, but Tim had yet to hand in his list of approved visitors.

I wrote letters, which take forever to get through to the convicts, and waited for Tim to call me. He didn't. But he *always* connects. I knew there was something wrong.

It required three days and numerous waits on hold, but at last a receptionist over on the mainland said, "I will get a message to Tim, at whichever facility he is in, telling him to phone his mother."

"At whichever facility he is in," means he has been moved to a different penitentiary. There is no other way of getting even this much information until your jailbird phones or writes and tells you.

Not ten minutes later my telephone rang. Tim.

He said one of the guards had delivered a message and an apology. Tim was to get in touch with his mother "immediately" and they were sorry they had previously told him not to call. In fact, they had told him he would be charged if he contacted his Mom. They had given the message to the wrong inmate. Lovely.

Tim was untroubled; he had already received my first letter and had realized this communication problem was coming from the sloppy legal system and not from home.

He is back in Brannen Lake Correctional, Nanaimo, and happily settled. Best correctional facility in British Columbia, now that New Haven in Burnaby is closed. The guys have to work hard all day and take evening courses. You can't go there unless you are willing to sweat and study. I wish he could stay for twenty years.

His arrest happened because he was being "disruptive and disorderly." Stoned in public.

Once they had put him under lock and key, they found an old charge not yet dealt with: the perfect excuse for a trial and a prison term. Never mind how much it will cost the taxpayers.

Tim told me about his trial.

The judge said, "This charge is older than the one that sent you to prison two months ago. Why is this being brought forward now?"

Then he said, "Since it has been presented, I guess we have to deal with it."

Offenders are offered a chance to speak up for themselves, but Tim has never taken advantage of this opportunity, before now. How I wish I had been there!

He got stuck with Mark Thompson for duty council, and Mr. Thompson had the crust to say, "Tim and his mother don't get along. They aren't speaking."

Tim stood up and came very close to calling Mr. Thompson a liar. He said he and his mother had an awesome relationship, saw one another at least once a day, and "take care of each other."

He said he was trying to manage with suboxone and he knew he had messed up but he definitely wanted to get back on it. He said it was "right" to plead guilty and he didn't mind more incarceration. He thought thirty days was fair. He told me the Crown, at that point, had already mentioned sixty days.

The judge said, "Mr. Spencer, you are an outstanding representative of yourself."

He gave Mr. Thompson a disapproving glare and he gave Tim thirty days.

Saturday, March 31, 2018

Church, for me, will have to be tomorrow morning instead of this afternoon. I was heading out the door for the 5 o'clock service when who should arrive but the ex-girlfriend with her sons. Obviously she knows when Tim is safely tucked away inside, although it wasn't mentioned.

She asked if they could stay for a while? ... and I can't see myself letting such a chance go by!

The twins pulled out the old dress up trunk and had a blast. Only two arguments: who got to have Opa's Canadian Coast Guard cap and who would be first to wear Aunty Elaine's graduation gown.

Their mother talked, mostly about what her children are doing. It was an entertaining visit, and almost like old times.

Wish I could quit wondering why this new friendship is developing.

James isn't wondering. He said, "She needs something; you will find out what it is soon enough. Meanwhile, take pleasure in your grandchildren."

Marvellous advice!

Sunday, April 1, 2018

This will be a peaceful Easter; all the kids are doing fun things without me. James and Elaine stopped in last Thursday, on their way to a week in Tofino. Kathleen is having an Easter dinner with friends. I'll be having dinner with other friends. Zan and Bedelia are in Port Coquitlam for the weekend and asked me to come down to their house on Easter Monday. My grandchildren will be getting their chocolate eggs late, but I don't suppose anybody will mind.

Sunday, April 15, 2018

Tim has been liberated—sent down island on the bus last Thursday morning.

We had planned for him to call me when he got back to town

and we would go to his bank together since I had his status card. The rest of his ID was lost when he was arrested; he thought bringing a witness to the bank might be helpful.

He got lucky: the bank had sent him a letter while he was locked up, using my address. This proved he was a member. They made him a new bank card immediately, and he withdrew a wad of money.

We had a delicious pancake breakfast at Good Neighbour. Tim paid our bill, added a five dollar tip and handed over an extra ten dollars "For the next customer."

I heard about the rest of his day that evening. He met Basil, his probation officer, in town and told him he would show up at the office later. He might have gone in the next morning ...

The missing ID was worrying him but then he met Rashelle, Ethan's girlfriend. Ethan is in the Victoria penal institution; he'll be there until June.

Rashelle had Tim's missing backpack and his ID. She lives on the streets where property must be portable, and she had been carrying his stuff around for three weeks.

And now we come to the ex-girlfriend. Well, Tim came to her car at the pool parking lot. Anybody can go in and swim but Tim and his ex are not supposed to connect. Anyway, he went in. The little boys saw him coming and froze in their seats. When the ex noticed Tim she was welcoming and she gave her sons permission with, "You can say hi to Daddy." They both ran to Daddy, and he got hugs and kisses and smiles and tears. My grandchildren are very carefully controlled. They are also polite and well behaved.

The ex said she wanted to have a talk with Tim. She off loaded the children, hopefully with their grandparents: she has been known to leave them alone at home. She came back to town and met Tim at the Library. It was about 7:30 p.m. when they parked in my driveway. The ex claims to be "Terrified of Tim," but apparently the terror can be turned on and off at her convenience.

Woocher was asleep in front of the fire and didn't bark. Tim and his ex thought we were out for a walk. They chatted for another twenty minutes. When I closed my blinds, Tim came in for food and a shower.

He said he had given his ex-girlfriend "time to vent." They have come to a huge decision: they can settle their family problems without benefit of any lawyers.

Basically, Tim is being set up because the ex can't find anyone superior to Tim's family lawyer. She is running scared on this one. And she can so easily talk him around to her point of view.

I didn't see Tim until the next day at suppertime when he got out various papers from the correctional facility and showed me his "Institutional Art." Although he has never had any training, Tim, more than any of my other children, has been blessed with artistic talent.

When he brought out the incredible pictures of birds and animals he had drawn, in the Coast Salish genre unique to the south coast of British Columbia, I said, "These pictures are fantastic! We can frame them, and the boys will love them!"

Tim has promised the twins gift cards from Walmart, where he is not entitled to go, and could Mom pick them up? I hate shopping at Walmart!

Wednesday, April 18, 2018

This morning, as Woocher and I were coming back from our walk, we met a pretty First Nations girl on the road behind my building. There are some mixed-race families living in our strata but no Indigenous folks come here except for Tim and his friends.

I said "Hi," and she said, "Tim is waiting for you on your patio."

I asked, "Are you Tim's friend? Come on back and have breakfast."

She did, and when we got to the patio there were Callum, Tim, and Rashelle, all three cold and wet and waiting to eat. I keep milk and cereal and fruit on hand for Tim; there was also a package of store bought hot cross buns. Tim went back to the fridge and got the cheese.

When all had been fed and warmed and dried, three of them needed a ride to Tim's campsite. Tim had his bike. I shifted the others down to the river, got hugs from the girls, and went back to find Tim still on the patio and overwrought. *Somebody* had stolen his new jacket ($200 on sale for eighty) and his headphones. He was totally stuck inside this thought; he truly could not move on with his life. I sent him back into the house to conduct a search. He found the jacket and headphones exactly where he had left them. Amazing.

Got the gift cards at Walmart and left those, along with the twins' pictures from Daddy, on their own doorknob instead of at Grandpa's. The bushes beside the house, left untrimmed, have leafed out; consequently their door is much less visible from the road.

The ex-girlfriend called to thank me for the boys' gifts, and to organize a drop off of slightly outdated groceries for Tim. It would have to be at 6:30 p.m., as the children were in after school care until 6, and she didn't want to come if Tim was there.

Tim never tells me when he is coming; he simply arrives. The ex planned to phone before she left home. If Tim showed up after her call, would I remove the bright orange pig living in the back window and then she would know he was there and drive on? She would see his bike! ... but with the ex there always has to be intrigue.

Tim came, wanting a shower and a meal.

I said, "You do your wash and I'll make you a supper to go because your sons are coming here soon and I know you won't want their fun with their Oma messed up."

Tim was more than willing to hurry, and would I make extra sandwiches for Dallas?

Yes, of course! As my father used to say, "I would be tickled pink!" I like Dallas.

I knew a lot about him long before meeting him. Tim often spoke of his friend, Dallas, who had something wrong inside (maybe cancer?) and used heroin to control the pain. When the river started to recede, back in the early spring, it was Dallas who spearheaded the clean up of last year's unauthorized campsite, preparing it for this year's unauthorized campers.

And when Tim invited him to come for supper and meet his mother, Dallas took the trouble to put on a clean shirt.

Supper that night, served on vintage Corningware plates, was the standard buns and cheese along with any vegetables I happened to have. That night we had sliced tomatoes and cucumbers and there might have been homemade baking powder biscuits. As usual, salad dressing and peanut butter were served in their jars; milk was served in its box; the pop was served in cans.

Dallas thanked me when he left, and added, "It was a real pleasure to have a formal dinner."

Tim and his ex-girlfriend didn't meet at my door but it was a near thing. Tim's cologne was still floating in the air and the ex noticed it instantly.

The children and their mother are learning American Sign Language together. Directed by a sign from their mother, they thanked me for dropping off their Walmart cards, but it was the pictures from Daddy they wanted to talk about. They had a lot of fun playing in my living room (until 8 p.m., God help me) and I endured, and the ex laughed and laughed. She appreciated her own puns although a few were in dubious taste.

In the old days, pre twins, she used to have an unlimited supply of suggestive humour. At family functions, we studied our plates with weak grins and eventually she spared us those kinds of jokes.

One surprise: she said, "Now that we are working on our relationship ... "

I guess I need to get started.

Tim says he is going for his suboxone regularly—I didn't ask. He said he had been in to see his probation officer—I did ask. And he said his PO is aware of the ex being back in my life.

Saturday, April 21, 2018

Tim's ex-girlfriend and the twins were here last night: their fourth visit. Tim hasn't been in for two days.

My friend Margaret has daughters acting in *Beauty and the Beast*. She has a ticket for me, and two extras and she wants to give the extras to Tim's boys. I'm almost certain the ex won't let the kids go anywhere with me, but we'll see.

Monday, April 23, 2018

Tim hasn't been seen for four days. One good thing: with so many citizens overdosing and dying in British Columbia, anxious parents and friends are being encouraged to phone the police non emergency number and ask about their loved ones. I called and left a worried message.

The twins aren't allowed to go to *Beauty and the Beast*—at least not with me.

Thursday, April 26, 2018

When I got home from *Beauty and the Beast* there was a message from an RCMP officer on my answering machine.

He hadn't seen Tim, himself, but he had found the camp and talked to other campers who said, "Tim is okay." He had left messages across the district for him to call his mother.

Tim phoned later from the homeless shelter. He *isn't* okay; I knew there was a problem when I hadn't seen him for so long. He has been hiding from the cops. He didn't say why, but told me he needs to connect with his lawyer if he can get to my place safely. He isn't allowed to make long distance calls from the shelter's phone.

He bought himself a new cell phone last Welfare Wednesday but, as usual, it had already been sold for drug money.

Saturday, April 28, 2018

In the end, I sent an email to the lawyer, telling him that Tim, in his usual vague way, thought he needed help as he was due to be arrested.

I told Stefano, "Sorry I haven't got hold of what I'm writing about, this time."

Wednesday, May 2, 2018

More trouble for Tim. There was a big fire in his campsite, and his tent, ID, bike, and other possessions are gone.

The couple camping beside him had built a shack made of recycled wooden pallets. Inside, they had a propane tank, guns and bullets, fireworks, and other interesting items. They started a fire at 4:30 a.m. and it was ten feet high in two seconds. An explosion, and the consequent crackling and screaming, woke Tim. As he ran out of his tent it melted and burned right behind him.

A big tree went up in flames and brought out the fire department. The police came, too, and they closed down the whole camp. Everybody has to move on.

Tim said, "Today I *really* feel homeless."

He came by for a long bath, absolutely worn out. He had no desire to eat, but I insisted and he was more relaxed when he left. Friends have been helpful; he had a borrowed bike and someone can get him another tent. I had an old backpack in the garage, waiting for an emergency. There might be an extra status card here if I can find it.

And most of his clothes live in banana boxes in my garage. His jackets and sweaters take up half of my coat closet. He keeps two large boxes on the shelves above. One is for odd socks; the other is for odd gloves and mittens. He tries for matching colours. He doesn't worry about matching styles.

Even with so much excitement, he is still hiding from the cops although they told me there is no warrant out. Evidently Tim has a guilty conscience. He is also in an emotional meltdown—aftermath of the fire and the consequent rumour. Word on the street: the fire was set on purpose to get rid of a girlfriend. Tim is personally acquainted with both parties.

He spent last night on my patio and slept around the clock. He is regrouped now, and ready to move on with his life.

Sunday, May 13, 2018

The ex-girlfriend lined me up to pay for laps for the twins' swim-a-thon and they were allowed to phone and tell me, "We did awesome, Oma!"

Their mother organized to collect the money last Friday; she was supposed to be here about 7:30 p.m. but planned to phone first, as the children had been invited to a birthday party. That was the last I heard until this evening. She called a few moments ago planning to come on Tuesday.

She and Tim meet in town occasionally and exchange a few words. The ex says, "It will work out, as long as the boys don't get confused."

Who decides who is confused? In my opinion, Tim's ex is one of the most confusing women I know.

Ever since she decided to be friends with me the family has been asking, "Why?"

Some thoughts:

The youngsters are getting older, and with doing activities such as this swim-a-thon they'll need sponsors. Family will have to be solicited; the ex-girlfriend has never had a wide circle of friends.

Her brother is newly divorced and his ex-wife won't tolerate his family seeing "her" little ones. Tim's ex is finally recognizing the deprivations Tim's family has been through.

The twins are putting in requests to see Daddy; they were too little to ask before.

The ex has started going to church.

She wants Tim back in her bed.

Sadly for me, I don't get any less nervous as we move along "working on our relationship." But my eventual goal is for Tim to be healthy, and seeing the two of us making efforts towards our original friendship is helpful for him.

Sunday, May 20, 2018

My grandsons have been trying to teach me American Sign. They think their Oma is a slow learner but I've got "Hi," "Come here," "Go Away," "Yes," and "No" mastered. The youngsters sign "Excuse me" when they want to leave the table and they can be reminded to say "Please" and "Thank you." A useful sign is, "Do you need to go to the toilet?"

The children are expected to keep their eyes glued on their mother at all times, so they don't ever miss an instruction.

Tuesday, May 29, 2018

Here we go again! Tim overdosed last Saturday, and his friends brought him back with naloxone. Then one of the friends noticed his infected hand.

This is a continuation of that horrible infection he had in his hand back in October. He never finished the last course of antibiotics; the hand wasn't totally healed and it remained puffy. Two weeks ago he was in a fight and split the knuckle. It could have used a stitch but that would never happen. The split is badly infected.

The friend who noticed the infection and saw the red streaks going up Tim's arm called a taxi and made him get in (How? I never could) and sent him off to Emergency.

The nurses put two drips into his arms. Tim told me one was an antibiotic and he thought the other one was for pain. Afterwards, he slept for about fifteen hours.

When he woke up he pulled out both needles and headed for the parking lot.

A nurse hustled along behind him, shouting, "Tim! Stop!!" Thank God he stopped, and the nurse caught up.

She said, "I could follow you by the blood squirts on the floor." He had managed to pop an artery when he messed with the needles. He went back inside and both drips were restarted. When he pulled them out again and left again they let him go.

According to Tim, since he wasn't there for an overdose he got better treatment than usual. I'm surprised they treated him at all; Tim is to the health system what sand is to an oyster.

He came in early on Sunday, shared his adventure and had breakfast. His hand was suitably protected by the dressing and wrapping put on at the hospital.

Then he came back on Sunday night with Gord, both needing a meal. Tim cooked them a pot of Kraft dinner. The hand was un-bandaged and disgusting.

As they prepared to leave, Tim asked if I would dress and rewrap his wound. When I was ready to start, he said, "Are your hands clean? You've been patting Woocher—you need to wash first."

I haven't seen Tim since Sunday night, but he was here sometime on Monday. He left his dirty laundry on the patio.

Thursday, May 31, 2018

Bruce and Alana have gone north to Haida Gwaii for a short holiday. I'm watering their garden on even dates, depending on the weather. Woocher comes too; he loves to chase their squirrels and roll on their lawn and drink out of their birdbath.

Woocher is allowed fruit and vegetables now, and his new favourite is frozen beet slices.

Tim appeared at suppertime, sick, vomiting, and significantly off balance. I gave him a Gravol and sent him upstairs to bed, but he came back because when he was lying down he couldn't breathe.

There are five big pillows on that bed. From the age of two, when his favourite teddy bear was used as an extra headrest, this son has needed more cushioning than anybody else in the family.

He went to sleep for a while, sitting up on the living room couch. There is no question his breathing is peculiar.

About 11 p.m. he started watching TV. This means he is feeling too lively to keep on sleeping but not yet energetic enough to start leaving.

He thought he might sleep again. I knew he wouldn't, but eventually Woocher and I went to bed. I set my mental alarm for 3 a.m. and discovered Tim gone and the door unlocked. I locked it. If he came back, too bad.

It's complicated helping with good choices when a person is chronically ill and also a night wanderer. And it's equally complicated discerning whether symptoms are new and I should worry, or drug related and will wear off.

Sunday, June 3, 2018

Another big conflagration in town. It was Kathleen's building this time—a four-storey apartment block with only three exits, no smoke detectors, no ceiling sprinklers, and the fire doors always being propped open by tenants who "need air." By good fortune, the blaze wasn't at her end. She and her dog got out with no trouble.

Nobody has permission to go back in. Kathleen and Pooh are staying with me until they can go home. The undamaged units are being opened individually, for folks to get their clothes and medications.

Tim has a date to start rehab (again) and hopefully circumstances will fall into place for him, this time. He is not in good shape: along with the odd breathing he has the whole Google list of symptoms for Hep C. He said he would go to the walk-in clinic with me. I hope he follows through but I will be surprised if he does.

Monday, June 4, 2018

The provincial emergency program for victims of Kathleen's fire is due to run out soon. Our local municipality is assessing whether or not to apply for an extension. Sounds like a no brainer, to me, with some residents unable to get back into their units until the repairs are completed. I hope there is a process established to keep the building owner working on the restoration. He didn't bother, following the last fire, five years ago. And we are desperately short of rental units in this town.

Woocher and Pooh are perfectly contented. But Tim has vanished. Sure hope he surfaces to claim his rehab bed.

Tuesday, June 5, 2018

Bruce and Alana are supposed to be on the ferry going back to Prince Rupert, but it was cancelled due to high winds. They are stuck on Haida Gwaii for another night. They found somewhere to sleep, a honeymoon suite no less! But they have to be at the ferry tomorrow morning at 4 a.m., so it is going to be a short night.

They said, "Sorry to hear about the fire in Kathleen's building. Please email and tell us how she and you are doing."

Thursday, June 7, 2018

Kathleen and Pooh should be able to go home soon. Their end of the building has both water and electricity turned back on, and today the doors and locks are being repaired. All of Kathleen's friends are safe and most of them can return. Nineteen units are uninhabitable at this time.

We have had a busy week, with a lot of meetings and paperwork for Kathleen, as well as two monitored trips into her unit for meds and other essentials. As for Pooh and Woocher, the neighbours aren't complaining yet.

Tim has gone to the Nanaimo Hospital. The plan: a week in detox followed by three months of rehabilitation at Comox Valley Recovery

Centre in Courtenay. The community outreach nurse conducted him to Nanaimo detox, and she will take him on to Courtenay next week.

Up until last night, I wasn't sure if this plan would work because Tim hadn't been in touch, either with me or the nurse, but he arrived here at midnight. Pooh barked at him and woke Kathleen. Since Woocher is used to activity on the patio and doesn't bother to address it, I slept right through. Tim spent the night on the lounger and was ready when his ride came. That's the good news.

The bad news for the last while has been Tim's health. He was already feeling tired and nauseated three weeks ago when he was coping with that infected hand. Then, about a week later, he started to gain weight rapidly. It really shows, since heroin has made him so skinny. He has enormous ankles and a huge belly and a double chin. He has to push his bike because he falls off if he tries to ride. Maybe he was willing to go to detox/rehab because he's feeling so dreadful.

I told the community outreach nurse about Tim's frightening symptoms, and she warned Nanaimo detox he might need an emergency bed before he needs a detox bed.

Anyway, I've just spoken with a doctor at Nanaimo Hospital.

Tim asked him to talk to me and gave him permission to answer questions. He said Tim has heart failure.

They have him in Emergency, at the moment, but will put him upstairs in a ward later tonight. The heart treatment will complicate his detox treatment but they plan to keep him comfortable with morphine for the first little while. They won't let him go to Courtenay for rehab until he is recovering from the heart issue.

The doctor said Tim is not in any immediate danger and they figure his problem is treatable. They aren't putting him on oxygen. He can have company.

Sunday, June 10, 2018
   It's 10:30 a.m. Just had my fourth call from Nanaimo Hospital…

Monday, June 11, 2018
   Last week, Tim was diagnosed with heart failure and safely tucked away inside Nanaimo General. Now he and his heart are back on the streets here at home.

   Our latest crisis started early yesterday, with Tim bound and determined to go back to his camp in the bush. Nanaimo medical staff tried to hang on to him. The rest of us did our best to persuade him to stay and when asked, refused to drive him home. Multiple calls were exchanged between key players.
   Mary Grace and I were planning an afternoon visit at the hospital. My cousin, Norma, who went in to see Tim twice daily, was at his bedside the whole morning and very supportive. Van and Elizabeth had been in to see him the day before with treats, and had promised to come again. One of Tim's Team had organized a TV for him.
   But when it was clear he was resolved to leave, regardless, another team member cancelled her own plans and transported him down Island. It was either drive him or see him hitchhike for miles on the freeway, because heroin was calling and he couldn't concentrate on anything else.
   When he got to my house, Tim threw a thick document-size envelope onto the kitchen table, grabbed a hunk of cheese, hopped on his bike and was gone, with scarcely a word to either me or his driver.
   The papers he left behind included a wad of directives from various doctors: low salt diet; continued care for his infected hand with a list of the necessary dressings and bandages someone would have to purchase; six medications for heart, blood pressure, fluid build up, and infection; lists of appointments to make and keep with miscellaneous specialists. There is no way a person who is sick and homeless could cope with all that lot.

I drove into town and stocked up on dressings and bandages and ordered the new meds—ten days' worth. I'd rather get more as needed, if Tim survives, than purchase a two months' supply and waste the taxpayers' money if he goes back to the hospital or dies.

Tim came knocking on my door last night, relaxed and mellow and wanting to chat. He said the damage to his heart was caused by crystal meth and cocaine. He asked me to set up his new doctors' appointments.

We did have one problem: that horrific nausea returned and gave him the heck of a scare. He had assumed it was a thing of the past. But a Gravol settled his stomach, and he had supper and swallowed his new capsules and tablets with no complaints.

He said, "I have to be careful from here on in."

I had refused to get one of the meds the Nanaimo doctor ordered—a second antibiotic. The pharmacist told me it is fatal if you drink any alcohol while you are taking it.

But Tim has assured me he doesn't drink any alcohol ever (I wasn't aware of the "ever") and the intake nurse said she thought it would be safe for him to have it. I will go back today.

Tuesday, June 12, 2018

Tim said he and I have a "creative coexistence."

He came in for supper and his pills last night and asked to stay and watch TV because he was exhausted. At 11 p.m. Woocher and I went out for our last little walk, and Tim had a shower. When we got back, he had decided to leave. He said going now was more sensible than leaving my door unlocked later.

Wednesday, June 13, 2018

I sent this message to Tim's siblings and saved a copy:

If any of you want to connect with Tim while he is still healthy, better do it quickly. His health is extremely precarious. Either his heart condition or an overdose could finish him off at any point.

He is still using heroin but has cut down a lot.

His disposition is mostly reasonable when he's at my place, and he is here more often than previously.

Thursday, June 14, 2018

Tim asked me if his ex-girlfriend knew about his heart.

I said, "I haven't told her."

Tim wanted me to phone her. He said he was too nervous to do it himself, but *he* would want to be told if the positions were reversed. He thought the mother of his children ought to know.

Since he would be present during the conversation, I made him tell me, beforehand, what he wanted me to say. But my main intention was to deflect the drama I knew would be part of the call.

I said, "Tim asked me to phone you. He is quite ill."

The ex said, casually, "Oh? What is it … flu?"

"He has heart failure."

"*What*???"

"He has heart failure."

"Oh my God! Where is he? Is he in the hospital?"

"Nope. He's been to my place."

"I'll get the kids into the car, and we'll be right down."

I said, "It's a bit late for me to be having company. Why don't you come after school tomorrow?"

It was 9:15 p.m. The twins should have been in bed, long since. Besides, I make it clear to everyone Tim doesn't live here, and where he is or what he is doing when he *isn't* here is not my department.

Tim's ex asked me what she should tell the boys.

"You could tell them Daddy is sick," I suggested, "and they can go and see him at Oma's house."

She added a pathetic, "Will this be the last time they see him?"

I said, "It could be, if Tim moves to China the next day."

Friday, June 15, 2018

Friday started at 3 a.m. with a knock on the door. Tim.

"It's raining and I'm sick. Can I sleep on the couch? I can't get up the stairs."

He came in, and settled, and we both dozed a bit, in spite of his loud breathing. Then the breathing stopped. No one will believe the speed with which I reached the living room. Still no breathing. I shook him and yelled. Nothing. I dialed 911.

A woman answered. She was bossy, loud, and efficient but clear instructions in the middle of trauma are beneficial for distraught mothers.

She said, "Unlock your front door."

I was not supposed to bother with Dog: the "victim" came first. But I put Woocher in the garage anyway, or there might have been more victims.

She said I should remove the pillows and roll Tim onto the floor. I started with the first pillow and he stood straight up and said, "What's going on?"…and the paramedics came bursting through the door, draped with their equipment. Tim was exceptionally weak; he looked at them and fell backwards onto the couch.

One of the men said, "Don't I know you?" and the other one said, "It's Tim!" Then he studied me and said, "Who are you to Tim? Why is he here?"

The younger man talked to Tim and the older one talked to me. Questions upon questions. Tim mumbles, even on his good days, and I find it interesting the way people start to shout if they can't hear. I stopped answering my questioner and sat beside my son on the couch; this helped him to speak up and soothed the shouter.

The paramedics spent a lot of time checking and double-checking Tim's heart and lungs and blood pressure. The readings were all poor but they weren't sufficiently bad to need emergency assistance. I did apologize for dragging them out unnecessarily.

At breakfast time Tim asked me for forty bucks. He said he needed a fix if he was going to have a decent visit with his sons later on. Sad, but true. He has never asked me for drug money before and I told him I would do it *this one time*, for the sake of the children. We had to go to my bank (another trip into town), and he only got a twenty. Unluckily for him, his mother has been informed regarding the cost of heroin.

The ex-girlfriend phoned me during her lunch hour. There are two kinds of heart failure. She needed to know which kind Tim has got.

The boys and their mother came at 3:30 p.m. Tim got here at 3:45. They had a splendid family playtime, the first since Tim left in 2015.
Before Tim came in, I asked his ex if she would consent to photos. She said, "Not if Tim puts them on Facebook."
I told her "No worries. Tim doesn't have access to my camera or my computer."
We caught many adorable poses and the first ten worked. The rest were black. James gave me a newer camera to try. Guess I'll have to start using it.
Tim had brought brand new felt pens for the kids, and they emptied out the craft cupboard on to the kitchen table. The family made pictures for each other, covered with glue and sequins and glitter, while Woocher and I went out for a walk. Then they shifted to the living room and explored the dress up trunk while I made supper.
When supper was ready I directed the youngsters to the table, hoping to give their parents a private moment if they wanted it.
Twin Two said, "It's okay, Oma, they're talking."
Helpful of him to reassure me, but sad to see the child taking care of the parents.

The ex-girlfriend told Tim and me about the twins' bad teeth. They will both be requiring an anesthetic to have their cavities and extractions of rotten baby teeth dealt with.

Tim has never had a voice in any grocery decisions; the ex-girlfriend's choices have prevailed. Minimum salads; maximum Kraft dinners; lots of cookies; constant apple juice.

While Tim was busy with his kids, the ex-girlfriend told me, "I didn't tell the people at work about Tim. They would have sent me home." She meant because she would have been crying so extensively! This from the woman who found excuses to keep a no contact order in place for years, and continually cancelled the boys' playdates with their father.

Mother and twins left at 6 p.m. and Tim was gone by 6:10.

Before long there was a call from the nurse at the overdose prevention site. She said there had been "an incident" and they had phoned for an ambulance for Tim. He wanted me to go to Emergency and meet him there.

The nurse said, "He is walking to the ambulance as we speak."

I wish I had asked about "the incident" but I assumed it was his heart acting up.

Different first responders, this trip. When I got to the hospital, one of them, a kind, caring man, came into the waiting room to talk to me. He said Tim had overdosed at the OPS and had fallen down their stairs.

I was allowed to go to the back and see him, but for five minutes at most, as the whole of the Emergency ward was extremely busy and overcrowded.

And there was Tim, sour and miserable, sitting on one of the extra chairs lined up against the wall. He wanted to leave Emergency "right now." He groused because they were "keeping him waiting," and demanded a ride to town. He said it was "only an overdose" and he didn't need to be there.

But he wasn't lifted into the ambulance—he chose to get in. Tim's

FASD was fully out front, here. I could tell he had lost track of the way consequences tend to follow actions.

And never a thought spared for the paramedics who had put themselves out for him, or for the cost of these services he suddenly didn't want but would count on if his heart started having more symptoms.

I said, "Your ear is bleeding."

The paramedic said, "I didn't see that," and he went for ice and a dressing.

I went home.

Monday, June 18, 2018

Tim has gone missing.

He connected on Saturday morning, even though I had walked out on him in Emergency the night before, and asked me to bring his pills down to the food bank because he hadn't enough energy to walk to my house. His bike was at the overdose site and it wouldn't be open until noon.

Sunday night he came to me for supper and his medications. He was stoned, but at least he was there. The ex-girlfriend had asked if the twins could come and see him sometime this week but Tim couldn't concentrate. He left laughing.

I haven't seen him since. He intended to meet me today outside the credit union, to get his medications. He was supposed to swallow those with his lunch at the food bank. When he didn't turn up, I took the pills to the food bank myself.

I'm still wondering what happened to him.

Possibly he met up with the ex-girlfriend and has been whisked off to her bungalow? She could easily have organized more meds for him; Tim knew the whole prescription hadn't been filled. And although having to work with the ex would make me a bit uneasy, if Tim is with his sons, he will be happy until he needs a fix.

Wednesday, June 20, 2018

Tim isn't missing. He turned up today at noon, very much under the influence, and wanting some lunch. He had forgotten about his pills. He had forgotten about his ex-girlfriend's birthday. He had forgotten about the previously planned celebration.

The twins came in right behind him, expecting a "Happy Birthday to Mommy" party. They proudly produced cards made in secret. Mommy admired them profusely but Daddy remained uninvolved; he was already falling asleep above his food. He finished eating, staggered to the couch, and slept the visit away.

The ex-girlfriend told me, years ago, "I always know when Tim has been using," but she didn't figure it out today. She thought he was having heart trouble and I didn't tell her anything different. Tim's face and ankles were visibly swollen; that helped.

She cried while I cleared the lunch dishes and the boys played with our old train set. She asked me for photos of Tim with the twins. How could I have any photos? We've had three years of "No Cameras!"

Then James and Elaine arrived, ready for dessert and birthday festivities, and the crying stopped.

Elaine is wonderful – she makes everyone feel important and special. She made much of Tim's ex, admired the kids' cards for Mommy, got us busy serving cake and ice cream, and built up the excitement with animal balloons. Uncle James, original owner of the train set, made an instantly popular cardboard tunnel. The youngsters were a bit shy at first, but they loosened up quickly. It's thanks to their Aunty Elaine and Uncle James they had a half decent afternoon.

Right after the twins and their mother left (and Tim didn't surface, even for a "goodbye") Kathleen called, to line up our dog walk. James and Elaine wanted to hear how things were going for her, following the fire. We could all have a nice walk together, but what to do with Tim?

We decided to shift him out onto the patio to finish his sleep. I put his shoes and backpack outside, along with a Coke and a big slice of birthday cake. James started helping him up ... and Tim awoke vigourously, energetic and furious. He stormed around the house, swearing, and slamming doors. I was thankful to have James at my back while Tim was exploding. Eventually he got himself out to the patio, onto his bike, and away.

When he was gone, I became intensely angry. So much energy for us, and not one speck for his sons. James was irritated, too. He said he could see why I dial 911 when Tim won't leave.

I have since calmed down, and Tim can come back without getting yelled at. Mary Grace, my ex-counselor, would have been impressed with all that anger coming from Ruth!

Friday, June 22, 2018

Thanks to Alana, Tim has his medications. What would I do without my family?

Tim hadn't been anywhere near me since the disastrous birthday party and I was not going to beat the bushes hunting for him. As a result, he had no heart meds for several days.

Alana volunteers at the food bank, and when Tim got there, this morning, he asked her to phone me. He said he was mad at his mother but he needed his pills because he was dying. He would ride out to get them if I would be at home.

I told Alana I doubted if Tim would have energy to bike such a long distance. And, quite apart from his health, when he is sulking he isn't fun to have around. I'm still in recovery following his birthday behaviour. It would be easier for both of us if a portion of his meds were living in town. I said I would be there in seven minutes.

Done!

Jill, who runs the food bank, has a small plastic vial of Tim's heart capsules and will make sure he takes them. She got me to sign a form, saying I had asked her to do this. She'll let me know when her supply is running low and I will get more, since Tim still isn't permitted to be within fifty metres of his own drug store.

Jill has a note I wrote for Tim. "Hope to see you soon for a nice cup of coffee and a chat. Love, Mom."

He'll be glad to know the door is open when he is ready to make himself visible.

Saturday, June 23, 2018

Around here it feels the same as when Tim first goes to jail—I just want to sleep. However, he could rise above his bad temper and show up at any moment. This is not as relaxing as a prison term, which ends on schedule.

Woocher is also exhausted; he just had a wash and a blow-dry downtown at The Doggy Bath. A bath is stressful because you never know who might jump into the tub with you. You have to pay close attention to every other dog, every second, especially the scary dogs that are bigger than you. And no matter how wet and soapy you are, if a new dog comes through the front barrier, it's your duty to growl.

The man I pay at Doggy Bath, Uri, was addicted in his youth and has been in recovery for many years. He has an adult son, regularly in and out of jail. Uri was in school with my kids, so we always have lots to talk about. I like being able to exchange stories with another parent—even one a generation younger than me—who is also nervous of street life and prefers the safety of incarceration for his son.

Thursday, June 28, 2018

Tim has finished being mad. He called twice, first to tell me another friend, one of the Rachaels, had overdosed and died and then to say he was at the overdose prevention site but was on his way to the hospital.

Shortly afterward, an OPS nurse phoned. She told me Tim was retaining considerable fluid. He had gone to Emergency with Rashelle and another street person who still owns a car; he had refused to go by ambulance.

The nurse said, "If anybody can make him stay in there, it will be Rashelle."

Excellent! No reason for me to be there, too.

Rashelle hauled along everything she owns—five full bags. OPS offered to store them but Rashelle said she is in for the long haul. This is the girl who kept Tim's possessions safe during his last imprisonment.

The community outreach nurse had a talk with Tim. She told him he has a serious heart disease but not necessarily fatal if he takes his medications, quits with the street drugs, and gets himself to rehab. Unfortunately, Tim is in panic mode and not doing thinking.

Monday, July 2, 2018

Tim called and asked me to bring him two of his heart tablets and would I mind making him a sandwich? I added in cookies and bananas and drinks.

It has been an unpleasant, stormy afternoon with the power going on and off. We met on my side of town because Tim thought the wild, uncontrolled traffic and the branches blowing across the highway would be, "too much for Mom."

He said, "I notice, more than I used to, if I forget my pills."

He has been talking to the intake nurse about rehab. He has been listening to a girl who shares his medical symptoms—she has a blood disease and Tim is sure he has it, too.

He might be using less heroin, maybe thanks to the big drug bust at the ferry terminal last week. He's been more talkative and much more thoughtful than usual the last few days.

Saturday, July 7, 2018

This was supposed to be an easy Saturday, with coffee at Bruce and Alana's at 10 a.m., and church at 5 p.m., and housework in between.

But then there was a request from the overdose prevention site. The nurse there had asked for an ambulance because Tim could barely breathe but he had refused to get into it. He said he would go to Emergency, but not with anybody except his mother. When I got there, he wouldn't budge for me, either.

Whatever he had used at the site had exacerbated his heart problem.

He was surrounded by friends who can't manage their own lives, and who were busy telling him what he should be doing while he fought for breath. Losing his temper didn't help him any.

We hung around, waiting for him to pass out; then he would have no choice regarding an ambulance trip. The nurse kept checking his blood oxygen levels and she had him on oxygen several times. After a while his breathing improved and he got on his bike and left, having apologized to me for the false alarm. His eyes were so puffy he could scarcely see. Two street friends immediately mounted their bicycles and rode on either side of him.

Wouldn't surprise me if another call comes tonight. Woocher and I walked at 6:30 p.m., 9:10 p.m., and 11:25 p.m., trying to forget ugly memories of Tim fighting for air.

Tuesday, July 10, 2018

Last Sunday Tim phoned from the hospital. Would I pick him up and take him to the homeless shelter? Our church was serving hamburgers at the shelter at noon that day, and I was assigned to the dessert table; for once details clicked easily into place.

Tim told me he had gone to Emergency late on Saturday night—by ambulance!!

"How did *that* happen?"

Tim explained, "My friends are persistent," and, "When I saw the driver I was willing to get in. She's one of the nice ones."

I said, "I'm nice too, dammit, and you wouldn't go with me!"

At the hospital, they had drained about twenty pounds of fluid out of him; he could open his eyes, and he desperately needed a belt. The doctors had given him a different diuretic along with a new prescription for his heart. He spent most of Sunday sleeping and peeing at the shelter.

Monday, when I got home from town, there was Tim sweeping sand off my patio! He made himself a sensible lunch, cleaned up, and swallowed his various tablets and capsules without protest. He remembered to give me the new prescription.

His bike had gone missing on Saturday; he discovered it this morning outside the overdose prevention site, parked in the bushes and unattended. It was back to being his.

Evening brought Tim's little sons and their mother. The ex-girlfriend is determined to be friendly.

They always come late in the day and are here long past what I think should be the boys' bedtime, but it's lovely to see the twins, no matter what the circumstances. The women talk; the kids play. There is seldom an opportunity for me and my grandchildren to have any conversation.

But while his mother used the bathroom, Twin Two said, "We were supposed to go and see Kelly and then we couldn't."

Twin One, his eyes shining, told me, "But then we came to your house. We like you better. Kelly is Mommy's friend."

Today started well. Tim came in for breakfast; he was in great shape and planning to meet a friend for lunch.

I handed in the new prescription at Tim's drug store and the folks there were helpful regarding my questions about changes. The heart pumping medication has been increased. Tim should have been taking it twice daily; it works for twelve hours. I usually see him once a day. No wonder we are in such a mess.

Anyway, because of being busy in town I missed Tim's frantic messages. His bike had been stolen! Not a surprise as it now has two owners. He needed to bring out a tire for the old wreck living on my patio, and he could hardly breathe and would I come and get him?

He was swelling up, and back to nausea and vomiting. We tried a Gravol. When his stomach settled, he nervously swallowed the new pill. Both seemed to help. He fixed up his old bike, showered, and went on his way.

Tim and I are on a roller coaster ride. We didn't want to go to the midway, and we didn't buy a ticket. But the roller coaster keeps on going round and round, up and down, with us on it.

Thursday, July 12, 2018

James and Elaine will be away for about a month. They sent a new email address, which I have copied and tucked away beside the phone. In case Tim's health goes sideways while they are gone, this is the address where I can reach them during their trip.

Monday, July 23, 2018

Every day the Addiction Daily News, put out by CCSA, pops into my inbox. One article, as my friend Clare used to say, was "spot on." I wrote to the author, telling her how much I had enjoyed her piece, and she actually answered! We sent several emails back and forth, and I saved them all for posterity.

An email to CBC:

> Thank you for your article 'More Supports Needed for People With FASD.' Every word is absolutely true! Our whole family lives the FASD disaster. And *we* have to be 'the lifelong support' for our son/brother, having discovered forty years ago there are few services out there. For the most part, volunteers are all there is.
>
> My son with FASD lives on the streets, but he comes to my place most days. He is a man with severe drug addictions, in and out of jail frequently. He has overdosed numerous times, and in early June of this year was diagnosed with heart failure. I write to his siblings whenever there is extra drama and have sent you their last few letters.

You are so right about the lack of understanding for folks with an FASD.

An email from CBC:

Thanks for your message. Reading about Tim's story breaks my heart, but I'm realizing his story is all too common. It's a real shame we can't do more for people with FASD, the same way our society does for others with brain injuries. It sounds like the overdose prevention site is a big help in Tim's life, is that here in Calgary?"

An email to CBC:

We live on Vancouver Island. I've often wondered how Calgary's street people survive in the winter. Here we whine if we get three cold days in a row.

Our overdose prevention site—we're not supposed to use the term 'Safe Injection Site'—opened recently and has already moved once because it got too small and because the neighbours complained. Now they've got it in the business section of town.

You are right; Tim's story is a common one. I'm in touch with several parents who have adult children with an FASD. We are going through crisis after crisis with our kids and we are getting too old to be parenting these permanent teenagers, but nobody else will take them on.

Articles such as yours will cause change. Please carry on. We need you!!"

An email from CBC:

> I'm happy to be a voice for people with FASD, I feel as if we are failing them as a society. It's tough on the streets in Calgary, it gets super cold and the shelters can barely keep up. We're getting safe injection sites here, and they're making a big difference. Small steps forward!

Thursday, July 26, 2018

Last week, there was a request from the ex-girlfriend. She thought it would be a good plan for Tim to make a card, or write a letter, for the twins to have "afterwards."

This is not an activity I will be organizing. Tim gets help with arranging treats for his boys whenever he asks me, and that's plenty!

I went up to the ex's bungalow yesterday with a loaf of my homemade bread. She reminded me to ask Tim to write a goodbye letter for the kids. Then she asked if I would write one too, since she knew I wasn't intending to live much longer.

The ex told me there was a warrant out for Tim to be arrested, and got weepy when I said, "Excellent. If he is locked up, he will be getting his heart medication a lot more often and his health will improve."

On the way home I stopped at the police station and found out there is, indeed, another warrant out for Tim. I told the young man at the desk about his heart failure.

"When he is arrested, you need to inform me *immediately*, and I will bring his meds to wherever he is."

The young fellow needed a moment to get hold of this unusual request.

"Why are you so involved?"

"Tim has brain damage."

"Why hasn't he got his pills with him?"

"He lives on the streets and loses everything."

"Will he be able to explain this to the arresting officer?"

"Yes, if he isn't high on heroin."

When he understood, at last, he put my information in the daybook and said he would notify all units at once.

I'm as bad as the ex-girlfriend, trying to control the lives of others. How many mothers organize their sons' arrests?

Saturday, July 28, 2018

Tim came in last night, stoned, bloated, and panting. I suggested another trip to Emergency—a waste of breath. He came back this afternoon much improved, having spent several hours in the hospital.

He said the police had walked into his camp, ready for an arrest, at 1 a.m. From out on the trail they could hear him trying to breathe. They told him he could either go to a cell at the police station, or he could go to Emergency.

He thought a choice was offered because, if the police had arrested him, they would have had to hold him for the whole weekend "and they didn't want a death on their hands."

For Tim, the hospital was not much better than a police station cell. Late in the morning he found himself with an objectionable nurse who made rude remarks about "natives" and "drug addicts."

When he got a bad cramp in his leg, she flashed, "Get up and walk it off!"

Tim removed himself from his IV and got up and walked off.

Sunday, July 29, 2018

My holiday dates are set! First to Cricket and Clay and the grandchildren in Calgary, August 15 to 21, and I am anticipating an easy, tranquil week with them. Then off to the busy Roman Catholic Church family camp with Bedelia and Zan and another set of grandchildren, August 23 to 26. Not sure how Tim will handle this, but Woocher has a spot lined up at the kennel August 14 to 27.

Because Woocher is on an anti-inflammatory for his bad leg, he has to have blood work at six month intervals. This time, he failed the blood test.

So then I had to collect an early morning urine specimen—with a ladle! It took me nearly a week, he was so nervous and so uncooperative. He kept backing up against bushes and fences instead of lifting his leg. Eventually, I cheated and gave him an enormous drink in the middle of the night. Collection at last!

And didn't he flunk the urine test, too. He has been put on another expensive medication for kidney disease, with a second blood test coming up at the end of August.

Tim is also being uncooperative regarding his meds, and two days without the heart-pumping pill bloats him horrendously. He came in on Friday, shaped like the Goodyear blimp, with both eyes swollen shut and an enormous 'spare tire' around his middle.

I had promised to go out dog walking with Kathleen, and I do have more than one child, and it isn't constantly going to be about Tim. I left him on my patio for forty-five minutes. He had lots of cold pop and ice water and cookies and comics and a chair in the shade.

When I got back he was lying with his feet on the patio, his body on the rocks, and his head on the road, and wearing nothing but a pair of boxer shorts. His elbow was bleeding, and he was groaning with each gasping breath. The neighbour living across the street from my patio was in an uproar.

My laundry rack, covered with clean clothes, had been knocked down. The lawn rake, broom, and shovel were spread across the concrete and my outdoor thermometer had become bits and pieces.

Tim wasn't responding, I thought, but when he heard me phoning for help there was lots of response and most of it rude. I told 911 not to bother, went into the house, and relocked the door. Tim got dressed, came wandering around to the front eating blueberries off the bushes, and knocked. Apparently we were starting afresh.

I said, "Hi Tim, how are you doing? Are you coming in?"

Tim said, "Hi Mom. Could I have a bowl of ice cream?"

When Tim came by the next morning, he was almost back to regular size. One diuretic works wonders for him. He must have been up and down the whole night! He put in a polite protest regarding my request for an ambulance the day before.

I asked, "If you had found *me* lying on the rocks, nearly naked, and bleeding, and moaning, wouldn't you have dialed 911?"

He said yes, but that was different.

These days, Tim needs his handful of pills no matter when he shows up, and too bad about Mom's Rules. But I'm not crazy about having him drop in late at night. We've decided I will routinely leave a supper and a tiny plastic bag of meds and a can of pop on the patio at 9:30 p.m. If he's hungry, he can come at his convenience any time during the night.

I thought this was working admirably. Not. Today Tim said, "Thanks for the suppers," but he hasn't bothered much about his meds. He says he usually needs someone to make him take them.

At least he has learned that much about himself.

Tuesday, July 31, 2018

A down to earth older nurse, Helen, who cares about Tim, works at both the homeless shelter and the overdose prevention site. I asked if she could give Tim his heart medications. She could.

She thought she would be able to keep his pills at the shelter, but if the folks there complained she would shift them to OPS instead. Either way, she'll make sure Tim takes one whenever she sees him. I do, too, and so does Jill at the food bank.

Helen said there are no side effects if you take extra pills, but there is a bad side effect (death) if you don't take all you need.

Wednesday, August 8, 2018

Tim is in trouble with the law again. He spent one night in a police station cell last week and was in court the next morning but then he was released to wait for a sentencing date.

Don't know the date; he might have already missed it. Don't know the charge, either. But it wasn't breach of probation. I checked in with his PO.

I wrote to Stefano, telling him this latest news, and added, "Tim is very ill; his heart is packing it in. He could use a long term in a correctional facility—or compulsory rehab: I keep on trying!—and somebody to make him take his meds twice daily. It's a miracle if I can get them into him once a day."

Stefano, bless his heart, wrote back right away. He said he was sorry to hear such bad news about Tim's health, and "I will be pleased to help."

He reminded me that we have again gone past the three-month limit. Tim will have to apply for Legal Aid.

He finished his note with, "Talk to you soon."

Monday, August 13, 2018

Tim called from the homeless shelter. He said he couldn't see to ride his bike and would I come and get him or bring his heart pills. I did both. We then went on to the drugstore for more meds to leave at the shelter.

I had never seen Tim so puffed up. Of course, this is what I say every time I see him. The hospital was not mentioned. Taking medications regularly was not mentioned. We did talk about the way I will organize the patio for him before I go to Calgary.

Tomorrow will be busy. Court at 9 a.m. Get the patio set up for Tim. Kathleen has asked for a ride home from the church, where she will be doing volunteer work, and will I take her to pick up dog food? Woocher has to be taken to the kennel early in the afternoon. And the rest of the day will be mine!

I've talked to the neighbours who can see my patio from their front doors. They expect Tim to be in frequently (I hope!) for pills and clean clothes. They have promised to dial 911 if they have any concerns, and not try to solve his issues themselves.

Tuesday, August 21, 2018

Just home from Calgary. We landed on the island, as scheduled, at 7 p.m. even though our Calgary airline pilot was very late.

When we were all on board, and waiting to leave Calgary, our pilot arrived at the airport in a *different* plane. He had to get off his and sprint across the tarmac to ours. Surprisingly, we still got in to Victoria on time.

Cricket organizes my flights, and whenever possible we go with Jazz. These smaller planes are my favourites—you walk across grass to the plane and climb the steps. No sore ears, either way.

Thursday, August 23, 2018

I spent yesterday cleaning up from my Calgary holiday and getting ready for the church camp. Missed Woocher, but there's no point bringing him home for a few hours.

Last night, one of my neighbours invited me over for a nice cup of tea, and we had a long, lovely gossip. While I was gone, an unknown woman who said she was "a friend for Tim" left a message on my answering machine.

She told me Tim was "totally sick" and wouldn't go to Emergency. Would I bring his pills down to the Stone Bridge? There were directions on how to get to the camp and where to park. She said "the boys" would come to the car.

No idea when she called. She didn't leave a name and had used a phone booth; I couldn't phone back. Checked with the hospital last night and again just now—they haven't got him.

He must have taken some of his heart meds while I was in Calgary or this would have happened a while back.

Bedelia and Zan and the grandchildren are picking me up at noon. Off to camp!

Monday, August 28, 2018

Sometimes I'm tempted to get a cell phone, but after this week, there is no more temptation. I don't want a cell phone! But I *have* saved a series of texts from the last three days.

> **Friday, August 24, 2018**
> Text from James to Zan and Bedelia 5:57 p.m.
>
> Tim is in the hospital, in the intensive care unit for an infection in his hand.

> **Friday, August 24, 2018**
> Text from Bedelia to James 6:54 p.m.
>
> Oh dear, is it bad? Will they be able to make him stay put? Your mom wants to know how you heard. Was Tim conscious? …and able to give somebody your phone number? Could you please let Mary Grace know?

> **Friday, August 24, 2018**
> Text from James to Zan and Bedelia 7:01 p.m.
>
> Somebody from the hospital called me. Tim must have given them my number. He should be there for a while. They told me he won't be able to disconnect, by himself, from whatever it is they have him plugged in to. I will let Mary Grace know.

> **Friday, August 24, 2018**
> Text from James to Elaine 7:10 p.m.
>
> Thanks for the phone number. I called Mary Grace, and she will go up to see Tim in thirty minutes. Yay!!

Saturday, August 25, 2018
Text from James to Zan and Bedelia 3:34 p.m.

    Visiting Tim now. His hand infection has spread to his blood, so he will be here two to six weeks, depending on how he reacts to the treatment. He is sleeping a lot but did wake up long enough to eat a little bit, today. Tell Mom Mary Grace has been in a few times to visit him.

Sunday, August 26, 2018
Text from Bedelia to James 5:15 p.m.

    We stopped to see Tim on our way home from camp. He knew who we were, but he couldn't stay awake. Your mom is going to the hospital later this evening. Thanks for taking care of everything here.

Tuesday, August 28, 2018
    Tim is still in the intensive care unit with a dedicated nursing staff who are keeping a close eye on him. He is connected to a heart monitor and is getting his usual heart medications plus an extra diuretic to get rid of excess fluid. But this isn't about his heart; that bit of him is fairly stable. No dietary limits—he can have potato chips and chocolate.
    The main problem: a flaring up of last year's septicemia in his hand. Tim has been on antibiotics often, since then, but he never finished his prescriptions and the basic infection was never halted. Now the contamination has travelled up his arm and flowed into his blood stream. He has had a lot of tests and the medical authorities are very concerned. He has a couple of IVs running constantly, and other tubes going in and out.

The doctors don't want Tim to go into withdrawal because of his congestive heart failure. They are keeping him on a little bit of opioids and will switch to suboxone as soon as his body can handle the change. This is the first time Tim has been helped in this way. He would have stayed in the local hospital last year when his hand was infected, and in Nanaimo Hospital with his heart thing, if heroin hadn't been so tempting to him.

He has to be kept extremely quiet and untroubled. Company is limited to unemotional family members, and visits must be five minutes or less.

I didn't tell the ex-girlfriend about his illness when she and the boys came over last night but I have warned the ICU about her overreactions. If her drama reaches Tim, his blood pressure will shoot up and so will theirs. Unless she hears about this from someone else, which could easily happen, I will fill her in when he is stable.

The first night he was in the hospital, a nurse talked to Tim about being kept alive on machines and being resuscitated. She asked him what he wanted. He said he wanted to live, but not be a vegetable, and he wanted to talk to his doctor about it.

They are aware of his FASD, but I'm not sure they understand what it could mean in terms of his illness and recovery. I will search my files for an easy list of adult symptoms. Most working people don't have time to read anything more complicated.

Wednesday, August 29, 2018

This evening Tim was sitting up eating dinner—if hospital food can be designated "dinner"—and he seemed a whole lot healthier than on Sunday night, except that his arm was still the wrong colour. We are allowed to linger a bit longer, as of this morning.

He seldom mentions other visitors, although I know Mary Grace and various family members have been in to see him. I went up twice, yesterday, and will go more often if he is having long stretches without company.

Elizabeth has been there regularly; Tim says her homegrown grapes are "Unbelievable."

The outreach nurse left me a message. She had gone to the hospital for a friendly visit with Tim and had ended up being authoritarian and telling him off. He was already setting limits on his stay, regardless of his condition. He thought he could go to my place. Not! His medical issues have gone way beyond anything his mother could do for him.

Thursday, August 30, 2018

Tim is a little better although not out of the woods yet. Six days in ICU. Now he has been moved to a regular four-bed ward. Even though his energy levels are pathetic, he's revelling in the change: increased action and other folks to talk to. He is getting an antibiotic drip at four-hour intervals, around the clock. His arm is enormously swollen, still a weird colour, and appears unchanged to me, but his lab work has shown a slight improvement.

He can have more visitors, adults only, and we have to wear the gloves and gowns provided. They suggest friends and family with kids don't come, as the infection he has is one of the worst kinds and easy to spread. They are keeping curtains around his bed at all times.

He is on suboxone and not desperate for heroin. The outreach nurse and the hospital social worker are trying to organize a hospital to rehabilitation connection for him. The doctors want Tim under their eye for at least another week. They are not satisfied with his arm.

Tim says the general atmosphere is "too much like jail." He is restless and wants to leave. Food is his main problem. He isn't getting enough to eat, even with all the edible gifts from his friends and family. I've got a TV for him, in the hope of keeping him contented.

Thursday, September 6, 2018

Tim is out of immediate danger, and this unpleasant episode (for him) is turning into an extended holiday for me. I'm treasuring my break from Tim's usual lifestyle and from his street friends. Visiting is much easier at the hospital than it was at the jails.

Tim's doctors have agreed to him having short strolls on the grounds and smoking the occasional cigarette. He has to wheel his IV pole along. I make us thermos bottles of coffee and packages of cookies; we procure a picnic table and savour the sunshine and a change of scene twice a day.

I brought Woocher to the parking lot. He and Tim had a joyful reunion.

Saturday, September 8, 2018

This was James's forty-sixth birthday, Zan and Bedelia's moving day, Kathleen's first experience of getting herself to the Exhibition and back on her own, and Tim's chance to vanish from the hospital.

I had a lovely interlude having acknowledged the birthday, avoided the move, provided transportation money for Kathleen's excursion to the Exhibition, planned one trip up to the hospital instead of the usual two and having been unaware of Tim's disappearance until he was safely back in his bed.

Tim wanted to go to the Exhibition for a few hours but it was complicated. A pass had to be organized through his doctor, and a driver/manager had to be found who was not his mother. I was willing to pay for entrance fees and food and games and rides, but I wasn't willing to be in charge of Tim.

Tim's favourite nurse from the homeless shelter said she would do the honours. She planned to collect Tim on Saturday morning. I said I would leave some money at the main desk on Friday night.

Tim was ready by 10 a.m. but his ride didn't show. When I contacted the ward later to see if he had been safely returned, his nurse said he hadn't gone yet but he was relaxed, watching TV, and not antsy. She assumed his plans had changed and he would be leaving any moment. I took Woocher for a long walk.

When we met at his bed, this evening, Tim said, "I've had an adventure! Let's go out to the pagoda for a smoke and I'll tell you about it."

Tim had left a note on his hospital bed saying he had gone home, "and thanks for everything." He slipped out of his ward when everybody was busy and walked to the homeless shelter. He said he was worried about the nurse who hadn't picked him up—he thought there might have been an accident.

No accidents, but there had been a mix up concerning the money. The nurse who planned to drive/supervise thought it was going to be left at the main desk at the homeless shelter. When it wasn't there, she assumed other arrangements had been made for Tim, and got on with her day. Meanwhile, the money was at the main desk at the hospital.

The staff at the homeless shelter wanted Tim to go back to his ward. He thought, having got out, he should stay out. But the folks at the shelter went over his head and phoned his hospital nurse.

She was firm. "The wound on his hand has to be dressed twice daily, or it will go septic. He is on a very strong, very necessary antibiotic, and he needs his heart meds."

His bed would be held until 6 p.m.

Tim agreed to go back, but asked if he could have a decent meal first? They fed him three large helpings of the usual spaghetti blah, ordered a taxi for him, and got him back to the hospital at 5:45.

He thought his nurse would raise merry hell (well deserved) but she was very relieved to have him back, and she had already organized to have his Exhibition pass changed to Sunday.

Everybody except Tim is determined to cooperate. All he does is be charming. A pleasant change.

Five more days, and all fingers are crossed. There is supposed to be an empty bed in the Courtenay Rehabilitation Centre next Tuesday morning with Tim's name on it.

Monday, September 10, 2018

Just had a very scary phone call from Tim.

Nothing more can be done for his heart; he will have to take his pills for the rest of his life. Suboxone is keeping his addiction under control. His arm has reached the stage where oral antibiotics and careful dressing changes will suffice. Decisions are still to be made regarding a skin graft.

This morning he was moved to a different bed in a different ward; hospital staff members have named it The Overflow. This is where they put the patients they are trying to shuffle out.

I started to panic. Only three more days till rehab. There are several old folks parked in acute beds while they wait for rooms in nursing homes. The hospital is housing them for weeks and months. Couldn't they hang on to Tim for an extra three days?

A number of the medical staff, thinking only of Tim's arm and not the whole person, felt he was healthy enough to go home. They knew his bed was urgently needed.

Others—his own doctors and group of his nurses—understood Tim's FASD was just as much of a health issue as his infection; they went to battle for him.

The hospital social worker nailed it. She said, "This is clearly worth doing. We don't want to get in the way of a successful rehabilitation."

Tuesday, September 11, 2018

What a storm! When I came back from visiting Tim, it was raining so heavily I could scarcely see the road. The lights were out at Central intersection, and drivers were attempting to use the four-way stop procedure. Dangerous—that corner needs a police officer when the power goes off.

Tim's doctor wanted to talk to me. He said he had questions about FASD. I was willing to answer as long as he would answer questions about Tim.

We almost lost him—and he almost lost that arm.

This afternoon, Tim was eager to get out and come to me for a night. He is tired of a sedentary life surrounded by sick people. I encouraged him to stick it out. His bed at the Centre is confirmed for tomorrow.

Wednesday, September 12, 2018

Tim has gone to rehab in Courtenay! Alleluia!!!

His detox is long over. He has already had two and a half weeks off drugs, thanks to being too ill to sneak out until his suboxone took effect. In the end he was firm about wanting rehab, and you can get there from a health facility much more easily than from the courts or from the jails.

The doctors and nurses have been, for the most part, wonderfully cooperative. The nurses on three different wards spoiled Tim with extra care and attention. He had huge support for his addiction problem in ICU when it counted most. And the staff found his visitors intriguing; the mixed race family, the easily recognizable community advocates, and the many educated women of late middle age.

For Tim, hospital food was a major problem because he didn't get sufficient amounts. I offered fruit and chocolate at first but later added cheese and crackers and bags of cookies. Elizabeth never missed an early morning visit, bringing him dew covered grapes from her garden. Alana came with an ice cream bar and watched with amazement as it vanished in three bites.

Mary Grace kept him supplied with soft pastels, drawing pencils, and heavy art paper. Having a TV helped.

We thought we needed to keep the controls in place until he said decisively, "You can all quit worrying. I'm not going anywhere. I *want* to go to rehab."

He was supposed to leave the hospital this morning at 10:30 a.m.

At 9:15 a courier service package for Tim was delivered to my strata unit. I popped the package directly into the car, along with coffee and chocolate cookies and was at his bedside by 9:30. We had our last hospital coffee break together, this one celebrating the end of eighteen days of misery.

He was already organized to depart, except for his wound dressing—usually a ten minute affair—and his new nurse started doing that at 10 a.m. She couldn't find the necessary supplies. She had to send an aide searching for the proper scissors. She took forever with the final bandage cover. Then papers had to be signed. It was after 11 before Tim could leave.

Meanwhile, the outreach nurses who were driving him to Courtenay had arrived much too early. But they turned out to be both interesting and amusing; we had fun getting acquainted. One of them, now recovered from her own addiction, has a genuine understanding of Tim's difficulties.

Friday, September 14, 2018

Yesterday my telephone rang nonstop. Calls from the family and from Tim's support network with everybody wanting to be sure he had gone to rehab at last.

Today two more officials connected: one was from the RCMP and the other was Tim's probation officer.

The police were worried. They had noticed Tim wasn't around a while ago and had been keeping an eye out for him. Then they had started actively searching and leaving messages with his friends. The street remained silent. Messages to "call your mother" are passed on. Messages to "get in touch with the police" are ignored.

The officer who phoned me finally became truly concerned, checked Tim's vast file, and called because mine was the only number she found. She was surprised to get a mother and delighted to hear where Tim had gone. She promised to tell her department, offered to let Basil know, and said she would call the Crown Counsel office. I said I had already been in to see the Crown and had tried to reach Basil but he was away on holiday.

However, Basil is back. He called first thing, needing to know which rehabilitation center Tim was in and how he got there. He said he would contact the outreach nurses and Comox Rehab Centre for a report.

I said, "Don't you believe me?"

Basil said, "I do, but the government won't. They expect me to do my own research."

Sunday, September 16, 2018

Not sure how the rehab center is going to get paid. Tried to find out how this works, but Tim is *so* out to lunch when it comes to money. I am assuming they are getting his whole monthly disability pension while he is there but can't confirm this as he doesn't seem to have a clue.

When Tim was afraid of rehab he said he would rather go to jail. Now that he is in rehab, he loves it, and has told me during two extended calls how delighted he is to be there. If he returns to drugs at least he will be willing to go back.

I am so relieved to hear he is happy and busy and not homesick.

Monday, September 24, 2018

Tim phoned me this morning. His news gets better and better. He went to the center on a twenty-eight-day program and has since signed up for three months. He is at ease with all aspects of his new situation.

There had been one problem and care was taken to keep it from me until it was sorted out, "because you always worry."

Between Tim's intermittent memory and the center's lack of awareness, nobody remembered the dressing on his hand until the second evening. The wound looked ugly; he was taken to a clinic for a checkup. Although he had forgotten to be responsible for his dressings, he hadn't forgotten his oral antibiotics and wasn't infectious. He could go right back to the center.

Now he has an appointment to see a dermatologist. Various doctors have suggested a skin graft; Tim will be seeing the specialist to find out what's next.

Two nurses from our local drug and alcohol went to see Tim last week. They invited me, but I already had commitments. However, I sent a big bag of clothes and two calling cards. I didn't find out about calling cards until recently; they are much cheaper than collect telephone calls. The clothes won't fit for long. Tim is quickly gaining back the one hundred plus pounds he lost to drugs. He said they eat six times daily!

Wednesday, October 10, 2018

A message from the homeless shelter—there is a big box for Tim at the front desk, an early Halloween surprise. I went down and picked it up. If that box is full of chocolate he will be sick for a week.

And a message from Tim—he is running out of felt pens and drawing paper; could I ask Mary Grace if she has any more? He also asked for clothes hangers.

I said, "How many?"

Tim said, "All you can spare." He plans to share them around.

Six meals a day at the center, but no coat hangers.

And Tim's wonderful, fabulous news—he won't be having a skin graft! When he went for a last check, before surgery, the doctor was amazed at the improvement in his hand: new, healthy skin growing around the hole. She was also pleased with his general condition. She decided the graft would be unnecessary.

Sunday, October 28, 2018

Last week Tim asked me for his ex-girlfriend's phone number and he has already spoken with his sons. He said he was nervous, going through the ex, and the kids were a bit shy but excited to talk to Daddy. That was his first call to the boys in three years, and why not? The no contact order is long past.

Bruce and Alana and I went up to Courtenay today and had an enjoyable afternoon with Tim. We met in the dining room and were given a tour of the whole facility. I found the men who live there polite, pleasant, and enormously supportive of each other.

Tim has gained nearly forty pounds, maybe more, and is very contented with life in the center. The problem is, someday he will have to come out.

The Sober Living in our town would work for him, but only if they would have a space when he needed a space. The Sober Living Centre in Courtenay, connected to the rehab center where he is presently living, would be a better choice. He could get in there directly from rehab, with no complications. But it is a long way from his sons.

The ex-girlfriend told him he could see the boys if he went to rehab, and he thinks she will stick to that promise.

Tim is responsible for his own heart pills; he says he is remembering to take them.

He told us, "If I forget, I notice pretty quick!"

He isn't smoking. Instead, he is doing something I've never heard of before—vaping. You don't go outside for a smoke, anymore; you go out for a vape. He showed us how it worked. He doesn't appear to be a man smoking, more like a big smudge of smoke in the middle of the lawn.

Tim sent home two summer jackets he doesn't need. When Woocher smelled them, he caught up his most dilapidated stuffed bear, and sat beside the bag, whimpering. Too bad Tim missed the show.

Thursday, November 15, 2018

Tim finishes his present rehab stint on December 11. He already did the paperwork asking for twelve months in the halfway sober living program.

He saw his counselor today and called to share his good news. He and two others have been recommended for Second Stage. The counselor is very pleased with herself and with Tim.

Second Stage is part of the same complex where Tim is living now, but he won't be moving for a few weeks because they are repainting the inside of that whole building. When he finally shifts across, it'll be the same staff, and other guys who are already friends. He said he might not stay for the whole year, but he is not yet ready to go back home.

He had more good news: Basil, his probation officer, has been busy on Tim's behalf. He connected with the nurses at Mental Health and Addictions, and at Drug and Alcohol, and at Overdose Prevention and he called Tim's counselors in Courtenay. Then he went to Crown Counsel with exceptional reports. Every charge against Tim has been dropped. His probation terminates at the end of November and he has no more court dates.

And with regard to his health issues, he asked me to connect with his family doctor here and organize a referral to Courtenay for him. Then his heart history and his infected arm history will be with his new doctor.

Tim will be having weekends at home, starting in late November, and we are all hoping to celebrate St. Nicholaas with him. It'll work, as long as we can get him back to Courtenay before Sunday night curfew. The Drug and Alcohol nurses might be able to help—they are still involved and plan to see him next Sunday.

The nurse who keeps in touch with me said, "So many of our lot talk about rehabilitation, and maybe go for a few days, and then they can't handle it and leave. Over and over again. And Tim, who was one of our worst, and seldom wanted to even discuss rehab, came out of nowhere. And here he is succeeding!"

Monday, November 19, 2018

Tim's first 'away' weekend is due—after eighty-nine sober days!—but he hasn't sorted out the bus system yet. He is assuming his nurse friends will be able to drive him one way.

I'm not so sure. Welfare Wednesday is coming up and nurses working with people who have addictions will be hard pressed. Most likely they will be mourning at least one loss before the weekend is over. Tim needs to consider taking the bus. Both ways.

The ex-girlfriend has promised to meet Tim on the Friday at my house where he can see his kids and make plans for the Saturday. He is excited. I'm not; I'm as bad as Tim with his bus problem. I'll have to feed the multitude something a lot more interesting than bread and cheese. Decisions are waiting to be made.

Sure hope it works out well. Sure hope he'll be able to come again for St. Nicholaas.

Sunday, November 25, 2018

The twins and their mother came for supper on Friday night. The boys spread Daddy's old toys across the downstairs. Tim helped them make a fort in the living room, with the furniture shifted around and blankets draped across. The ex-girlfriend worked with little Christmas crafts on the kitchen table and talked to me. We all had fun, and Tim did the whole cleanup.

They tried to organize an outside playtime for the next day, but the ex already had a busy Saturday planned.

I said, "Make it easy for yourself. Come for supper tomorrow night. Tim can make spaghetti."

Tim had a busy Saturday, with shopping and cooking, and he was thrilled to be seeing his sons twice on one weekend.

The Saturday visit was not so successful.

Tim's spaghetti dinner was delicious—with a salad to die for. The ex-girlfriend brought the same craft project, but this time she had decided to be The Overseer. She carried her tiny bits and pieces into the living room, where she sat on the carpet and tried to work on the low coffee table while Tim and the children played games around her and made another fort. I stayed in the kitchen—there was a mountain of dirty dishes.

After a while, the ex told Tim she needed a smoke and he got his vaping paraphernalia and they both went outside, with the questionable ex first assuring her boys, "Don't worry. You will be okay with Oma. She won't hurt you."

They came back flushed and angry. The trip outside wasn't to smoke but to demand money. And why? … there isn't any. Tim has already signed his Band money over to the ex, and most of his disability cheque goes to the Centre. He can afford to vape—I guess that's what the ex was noticing.

We finished the visit with the ex being, in Tim's opinion, "a little bit unkind" to one of the twins. Have to admit I didn't notice anything, but Tim did, and he was upset about it.

Later on, he said he couldn't understand why he was disturbed. This kind of behaviour on the part of his ex wasn't anything new. And it had usually been Twin Two not quite measuring up and being pointedly ignored.

The ex told Tim she hasn't yet decided about joining the family for St. Nicholaas. If the kids were a bit older, I could do a big push with lots of "Do you remember…?" but there is no point. They don't remember.

Wednesday, December 5, 2018

Boterkoek has been baked—twice. The second batch didn't burn. Pepernoten are done, and I burned the outside edge of one pan. Chocolate letters are wrapped. I need to get down to the post office and mail a St. Nicholaas package to Calgary. Smoked sausage and sauerkraut have been purchased and I'll prepare my part of the dinner on Saturday because Zan will need the stove for his nasi goering on Sunday. St. Nicholaas candies and chocolate coins are still waiting to be organized.

I plan to get Tim to string the outside lights, decorate the crab apple tree, help me shift tables and chairs around, and put up my inside Christmas tree. Maybe.

No notion if the twins are coming. Their mother has suddenly gone back to denying Tim access, unless she or a professional supervisor is present. Once again, their Oma doesn't cut it.

Tim isn't bothered by her rules; he is willing to jump through any number of hoops as long as he can see his sons. But how is he supposed to organize and pay for outside supervision?

And these are the two who decided they could manage without a lawyer.

Saturday, December 15, 2018

After many emails back and forth, connecting with the Centre, it seems Tim can't leave until the twenty-third. Which was what I wanted, so why the confusion? The confusion is because I had already booked his bus ticket for December 20, which was what *he* wanted.

Changing a bus ticket can only be done online and I didn't have the little icon to press for Change/Cancel.

After many more emails back and forth, connecting with the Island Link Bus Service, a kind soul there did magic and made it work out: the date and the money both got shifted, although I never did press Change/Cancel.

I sent Island Link a heartfelt thank you, and "I'm too old for this; it wears me out!"

Tim will have a whole week at home. He goes back on the last day of December, just in time for the Happy New Year festivities at the Centre. Perfect for me because a new year is an event I have no interest in celebrating.

Thursday, December 27, 2018

Kathleen had a huge disaster. Pooh got attacked at the park, "And half his ear is missing and he's covered with blood!!"

She managed to find a vet—on Christmas Day—and with the next call to me it was "a little cut but it has to be stitched," and she wouldn't leave him, not even for Christmas dinner at her Aunty Alana's place.

Pooh's problem caused Alana to have a small disaster. She couldn't understand Kathleen putting Pooh ahead of her dinner.

Bruce said, "This is not about your dinner; this is about a dog's ear." Then she could laugh and let it go. The rest of us, especially Tim, thoroughly enjoyed Alana's dinner.

Tim and I are managing nicely. He helps around the house and otherwise keeps himself busy. He never stops smiling; it's wonderful!

The ex and her sons came to us late on Christmas morning. They had school made crafts and homemade cards for Daddy, and Tim had presents for them. It was a happy visit. The ex said they would be able to come again before Tim goes back to Courtenay.

2019 – Emails

Tuesday, January 1, 2019

Hi Mom
In case you didn't get my message … I made it back. I shared the shortbread and the ginger cookies. They were a hit. Everybody loved them. They thought I made them. You haven't lost any talent. Thank you again for the best Christmas Holidays I have had in years. It was awesome being Sober. Happy new Year!!!

Thursday, February 14, 2019

Hi Mom
Hope all is well. I am doing great. Would like to come down Feb. 27 Wed.—Mar. 6 Wed. Is that OK? That way some of it is weekdays and I hope to see about getting another status card. And it'll be your birthday, and I am going to see if I can see my boys at a park on Sunday. The 10:30 bus (I think that was the time you said) that works for me. If there is snow I can walk to your place, no problem. Will pack light. Hopefully that works for you. I am going to my Doctor's today for prescriptions renewal, and get carries for those days for suboxone. Have a good day.

Monday, February 18, 2019

Good morning Mom

I talked to the ex on Sunday. I told her I was coming down for your Birthday and said I'm hoping to see the boys on the weekend at a park again. She said that yes we could figure it out. I told her I would talk closer to the date. See you on Feb 27.

My doctor here has started my treatment for Hep C.

Wednesday, April 3, 2019

Hi Mom

Had a meeting with Courtenay Mental Health, about leaving Comox rehab and living at the Sober Living Centre at home. I got approved. Yay! But I have to meet with the man from Sober Living when I come down. I told him I was coming from April 10 to 17. I have to call him when I get to town. He seems to be a friendly guy. I am excited about this.

The people here said, worst case scenario: if I slip up, they will be happy for me to come back. That's pretty decent of them.

Thanks again and see you soon. Hope you have a good day.

Wednesday, May 1, 2019

Hi Mom

I went to my new doctor about my Suboxone and a lady who works in the office recognized me.

(It's nice to be back home.) We got to talking and she wanted to know if I would be interested to work as an outreach worker a couple days a week (paid work). I said a big yes. So she is going to talk to the doctor and see if it can be done. I am totally stoked about it. Things are falling into place for me. Sobriety rocks. Maybe I can help others change their lives. Cross your fingers for me.

Wednesday, May 15, 2019

Hi Mom

I had a rough day doing outreach. I ran into two of my old friends that went to rehab and both ended up back on the streets. One had two months clean and the other six months. Both of them said their mistake was coming back to town. It sort of unsettled me to see them in rough shape.

Then I came across another friend with mental problems trying to shoot up right on the corner in town. He got mad cause he couldn't find his vein. He was cursing and swearing, asking people to help him. Poor guy. He almost asked me but he remembered I was clean and told me I won't ask you for help cause you are clean. Never mind the strangers he was asking. Welcome to the street life. I am so happy and blessed to be out of that scene. It never bothered me before, all this drama. I had to vent. Sorry to dump the reality on you, Mom. Just wanted to relieve some mental pressure. Thank you.

Saturday, May 25, 2019

Hi Mom

Yesterday was my Nine Month sobriety date. I feel amazing. I never thought I would ever see a *week* of sobriety, let alone nine months. I treasure life more and more every day.

Reflecting on my life and I want to say I am sorry for the stress I have caused you and the family up until nine months ago. A sorry doesn't seem like much to me. But what I can do is live a positive, productive life.

Thank you for being the best mom ever. You were always there for court, hospital, jail and any other problem I got myself into. You are the biggest support in my network. I wish that I had made this choice sooner. I wanted to let you know that I appreciate everything you have done. Here's to another nine months. I love my future!

Appendix I

I was asked to write an article for the 1999 Christmas edition of *Special Families*. For me, at that time, St Nicholaas was much more interesting than Christmas. Tim offered to help. We named our piece "Celebrating St. Nicholaas."

Celebrating St. Nicholaas

Every year my mother puts a big effort into gathering the whole family for an early December St. Nicholaas party. My father is Dutch Canadian; for my mother, and for us, the Feast of St. Nicholaas has always been a unique cultural event.

When we were little, St. Nicholaas Eve was one of the most exciting nights of the whole year. At bedtime, we arranged our shoes, full of carrots for the Saint's white horse, in front of the fireplace. Next morning the carrots were gone and our shoes were overflowing with presents. Toys and books, candy canes and oranges, pepernoten and speculaas, fashionable school supplies when we got a little older, and always a chocolate letter.

Chocolate letters (mine was a 'T' for Tim) were a very special reminder of St. Nicholaas's personal knowledge regarding each child. We found them tucked underneath our shoes, placed there by Black Pete, who brought the gifts down the chimney.

This event doesn't include carrots in our

shoes, any more, now us kids have grown and moved out, but Mom still puts up the St. Nicholaas decorations. She still bakes pepernoten and rolls truffles; she still makes stamppot with smoked sausage for dinner, and boterkoek for dessert; she still ties green ribbons around red and white peppermint candy canes. And we still celebrate with chocolate letters, wrapped in St. Nicholaas paper.

My mother says her main motive, nowadays, for carrying on our St. Nicholaas traditions is her need to bring the family together before Christmas. Most years we are waiting for December court dates, and my mother is afraid we won't be with each other at Christmas. Most years, she expects to be visiting in a prison on Christmas Day.

I'm the one who might be in jail. I've spent three Christmases there, already, and I'm only twenty-four. It seems like whenever December comes, I'm waiting to go before a Judge. Sometimes my trials are held over until January; sometimes I get conditional sentences that can be served in the community; sometimes, sure enough, I'm inside.

But last December I was clean. No recent crime, no court date, no curfew, nothing except an extended probation order. It was a Christmas to look forward to; maybe even a Christmas to prepare for, except I'm not talented at organizing.

We celebrated St. Nicholaas as usual. Mom and Dad and Grandma were there, and my sister, and us four boys. My mother says "One friend each," so three of us brought our women.

Family functions at my parents' house finish pretty early. The folks are getting old, I guess. Me and Sorrel, (she's my woman) and Red, an old school friend with lots of problems, went out with some other people after the party. A few drinks, and we began to realize we needed money for family Christmas presents. A few more drinks, and we suddenly knew a fantastic way to get hold of all the money we would need.

Sorrel's family held the cleaning contract at the local radio station. She worked there with her cousin most weekends. I helped out when there was nothing else to do, and had a good look around. The building had no alarm system and no dead bolt. Red and I could break in easily. Once in, it would be simple to remove the lighter, more expensive equipment. Radio station stuff is hard market on the Island, but I know an awesome fence. He travels; he can sell anything.

The most difficult part of the plan turned out to be getting Sorrel to cooperate, but she didn't have to do anything except drive. It was a cold, wet night and we didn't want to walk through town. Walking in the dark is spooky because you never can tell who you might meet, and you don't see their faces until it's maybe too late. And anyway, we would need a vehicle afterwards. We couldn't carry much stuff away.

When we had talked Sorrel into coming, and had polished off another beer, it was time to go. We thought we had organized fairly well; unfortunately our planning had been done in front of friends who figured they owed us one. As we left for the radio station, they called the cops.

Sorrel dropped us off at a deserted corner of the building, planning to return in about twenty minutes. We thought it would take that long to break the door lock, pack the multiplay compact disk machines into duffel bags, get ourselves out of there, and hide the bags in the bushes, if necessary.

Everything went according to plan, until we ran out of the damaged door, carrying our heavy bags. Without any warning, a cop appeared from behind a tree, and told us we were under arrest. He said our names, too. It was a dark night, and there were no streetlights, but he already knew who we were.

He had to catch us to arrest us, though. Red kept him busy for a while, but he caught me almost immediately. I can't run fast since my ankle broke last summer.

Sorrel did a drive past on the highway. She saw the cop car parked around the corner from the radio station, and knew we'd been busted, but she came back, anyway. She got busted too. The cop, already hiding behind his tree before we got there, had watched her dropping us off and had taken her licence number.

At the police station we were charged, booked, and searched. I lost my chocolate letter, and Sorrel lost her candy cane, still tied with green ribbon. Red had the last of my peper-noten in his pocket; luckily he'd eaten most of them. We celebrated the rest of St. Nicholaas

Eve in separate cells, with no talking allowed, and it was boring, but at least we weren't hungry. Tasty Dutch cooking sticks to your ribs.

                                        by Tim and his Mom.

Appendix II
Disabilities of Fetal Alcohol Spectrum Disorder

Typical brain-based, primary disabilities of Fetal Alcohol Spectrum Disorder can include:
- inconsistent memory and recall
- impulsivity, poor judgment, and the need for instant gratification
- difficulty shifting from one context to another
- inability to see another person's perspective
- inability to filter out environmental or emotional distractions and sensory stimuli
- slow and inconsistent cognitive and auditory processing
- decreased mental stamina
- difficulty interpreting and applying abstract concepts (for example, managing money and time)
- inability to predict outcomes (of their own or others' actions)
- resistance to change
- inability to recognize indirect social cues
- widely varying levels of maturity in different areas of development such as expressive language and language comprehension, social and self care skills, and awareness and regulation of emotions
- permanent vision and hearing problems; poorly developed bones, limbs, and fingers; organ damage

Secondary disabilities are not present at birth but may occur later in life as a result of the primary disabilities associated with FASD including:

- alcohol and/or drug problems
- mental health problems (including depression, panic attacks, mood swings)
- disrupted school experience (suspension, expulsion, and/or dropout)
- poor academic achievement and school failure
- low self esteem, high risk behaviour, easily victimized
- involvement with the law (trouble with authorities, charged and/or convicted of a crime)
- problems with employment
- uncooperative dependent living
- confinement (inpatient treatment for mental health; rehab; incarceration)
- sexually deviant behaviour

Appendix III
Glossary of Acronyms

B and E	break and enter
BCID	British Columbia Identification Card
CBC	Canadian Broadcasting Corporation
CCSA	Canadian Centre on Substance Abuse and Addiction
ECG	electrocardiogram
EMP	Electronic Monitoring Program
FASD	Fetal Alcohol Spectrum Disorder
GP	general practitioner (medical doctor)
GST	Goods and Services Tax
Hep C	Hepatitis C
ICBC	Insurance Corporation of British Columbia
ICU	Intensive Care Unit
IQ	intelligence quotient
IV	intravenous therapy
MBNA	a leading provider of credit cards
MLA	Member of the Legislative Assembly
OD	overdose
OPS	Overdose Prevention Site
PO	Probation Officer
RCMP	Royal Canadian Mounted Police

Appendix IV
Recipes from My Dutch Sister-in-law

Gevulde Boterkoek

5 eggs (or more. You will need 1 cup of raw egg)
4 oz ground almonds
½ cup sugar
1 tsp grated lemon rind
1 tsp almond extract
4 cups white flour
1¾ cups sugar
⅘ lb butter

Put eggs in a small bowl and beat with the almond extract. In another, slightly larger bowl put the ground almonds, the half-cup of sugar, and the lemon rind. Mix with just over half the egg mixture. Put aside.

Make a loose dough with the flour, sugar, and butter, and the rest of the egg mixture. Divide dough in half.

Spread half in a greased and floured 9" x 13" pan. Press down flat and even. Put the filling on top and spread it out into the corners of the pan with a wet rubber spatula. Sprinkle the second half of the dough evenly on top of the filling. Bake for one hour at 325°F.

Pepernoten

2 cups honey
1 cup sugar
1 egg
½ cup butter or margarine
¾ cup hot water
½ cup finely chopped nuts or sunflower seeds

3 tsp cinnamon
1½ tsp ginger
¾ tsp cloves
1½ tsp baking powder
½ tsp baking soda
7½ cups white flour

Cream honey, sugar, butter, and egg. Add hot water, and then all the other ingredients. Roll in long sticks, about ½ inch in diameter. (Finger width.) Freeze between layers of dish towels. The next day, slice the long rolls into tiny circles about ⅜" each—like little hockey pucks—and place flat on greased baking sheets. Spread them out—don't let them touch each other. Bake at 375°F for about 7 or 8 minutes. Turn the pan and give them another 7 or 8 minutes, carefully. Pepernoten harden as they cool and ripen in a few days. Store in a closed container with a tight lid.

Truffles:

¼ cup butter
2 tbsp cocoa powder
1 cup icing sugar
chocolate hail

Mix butter, cocoa, and icing sugar together into a lump. Taste. If the cocoa dominates, add a bit more icing sugar. Roll into small balls. Roll the balls in chocolate hail. If the hail won't stick to the balls, add a bit more butter to the original lump.

Keep finished truffles in the fridge.

Appendix IV
Life in the Trenches

Electronic Monitoring and FASD:
An adoptive parent's perspective[1]

There is one thing we can be certain of: our young people with FASD will always be bringing new, interesting occurrences into our lives. So far, we have been introduced to school suspensions; the legal system and Corrections; addictions; suicide attempts and the psyche ward; the damage dealt out by drug dealers along with several emergency surgeries; evictions and street living; unpleasant sexual diseases; many girlfriends, some of them pregnant.

Last November brought another crisis and initiated us into several brand new experiences within the space of a few weeks. The incident started in the usual way: a poorly planned B and E followed by a group arrest, several charges, a night in a cell at the local police station with one phone call allowed, an appearance before a judge the next morning, remand in custody, a plea of "Guilty" three weeks later, and incarceration.

The B and E had been done at a commercial establishment after hours, which is not quite so bad as breaking into a home where there might be people. But because a breach of probation was included in my son's charges, the Crown Counsel decided to ask the judge for two years less a day. (A sentence of more than two years means a federal prison.)

My son has a supportive lawyer who welcomes parental involvement. He appreciates any up to date information I can offer that might help the judge come to a better understanding of my son's problems. This time, an article I had written about FASD for a local

---

1 First published in 2001 by SNAP Newsmagazine Volume 16 Number 2

magazine proved to be very helpful. The sentence was four months in jail.

The next change in an otherwise more or less routine event was a phone call, two days later, from the Vancouver Island Regional Correctional Centre. My son's paperwork had actually travelled with him, for once, and it included the judge's copy of the magazine article. The Electronic Monitoring Program people had already reviewed his case and they wanted my opinion on the advisability of putting him on a monitor.

I said, "This isn't fair," and, "I don't know anything about electronic monitoring," and, "I don't want to be involved in these kinds of decisions; I only want to be the mom." (Because, while a "no" would infuriate my son, a "yes" that didn't work out would leave me feeling guilty forever.)

But my list of private doubts was extensive:

Being 'out' on EMP would mean a compulsory fixed address and a home phone. These were available to my son only at his own apartment, the very community from which his little group had emerged to do their B and E less than four weeks before.

This tiny, one bedroom apartment had two couples in permanent residence—my sons and their girlfriends—with, during the winter months, wall to wall carpet surfers. Being 'out' on EMP would mean no drugs or alcohol on the premises at any time. Could the whole group manage a clean and dry Christmas and New Year? …or the restrictions of a curfew during the holiday season?

And Christmas seemed to me a particularly bad time to start someone on a brand new lifestyle. Drug and Alcohol programs were gearing down; the schools for adults were already closed; all the services my son would need to access immediately had skeleton staffs in place. What would he do with himself during the next two weeks?

I expected electronic monitoring to be an extended punishment for all concerned. I didn't understand that it would provide some of my son's most fundamental needs—support, structure, and supervision.

The basic expectation of the EMP is normal behaviour: keep appointments; tell somebody where you are going and when you will be back and follow through; be home at a sensible time and in good condition; control your fists and your tongue. The people who programmed the monitor were friendly, fair, and reasonable. Many behaviour checks happened, and daily telephone contact was expected. My son understood that instant consequences would follow unprogrammed behaviours. One slip up, and he would be right back in jail.

His apartment community wanted the program to succeed and they cooperated with the new rules to the best of their ability. Because he had empty time on his hands, my son began to keep the apartment clean and tidy, and to cook the evening meal for everybody. With his usual night wandering eliminated, and with the regular exercise of walking to many daytime appointments, his disposition and his relationships (even his relationship with his cat) improved dramatically. Whenever I saw my son, he was smiling.

I said, "This monitor is the best thing that ever happened to you. I wish you could stay on it for the next thirty years."

Electronic monitoring worked because it provided constant supervision. It was a wonderful experience for our whole family, a success story for my son's peer group, and a proud victory for my son.

About the Author

Three adopted children with Fetal Alcohol Spectrum Disorder plus fifty years as a parent advocate have made Ruth Spencer an authority on the subject of FASD behaviours, even though she describes herself as "Just an ordinary mom with no letters after my name."

In 1994, at the request of other parents in her FASD support group, Ruth started to write about the challenges involved in loving, accepting, and supporting her older teenagers with FASD. There were long hours in Youth Court where "Everybody but me understood the system." There were visits to jails: "Once I was locked in the washroom by a guard with a real gun in his belt." There were many trips to Emergency, evictions, street living, sexually transmitted diseases, a crisis pregnancy, alcohol and drug abuse, overdose, welfare fraud, psyche ward stays and suicide. Ruth never ran short of new material. By 1997, her articles and poems were being published in Canadian magazines. *The Thirteenth Overdose* is her second full-length book.

Now a grandmother, Ruth is still parenting her adult children with FASD.

Made in the USA
Monee, IL
15 April 2021